TALK RADIO AND THE AMERICAN DREAM

Library of Congress Cataloging-in-Publication Data

Levin, Murray Burton.
Talk radio and the American dream.

Includes index.
1. Public opinion—United States.   2. United
States—Social conditions—1960–1980—Public opinion.
3. United States—Politics and government—1945—
Public opinion.   4. Talk shows—United States.
5. Trust (Psychology)   I. Title.
HN90.P8L48   1987   303.3'8'0973   86–45336
ISBN 0–669–13216–0 (alk. paper)
ISBN 0–669–13217–9 (pbk. : alk. paper)

Published simultaneously in Canada
Printed in the United States of America
Casebound International Standard Book Number: 0–669–13216–0
Paperbound International Standard Book Number: 0–669–13217–9
Library of Congress Catalog Card Number: 86–45336

The paper used in this publication meets
the minimum requirements of American National Standard
for Information Sciences—Permanence of Paper
for Printed Library Materials, ANSI Z39.48–1984.

86 87 88 89 90 8 7 6 5 4 3 2 1

To
JOSH *and* JAKE,
JESS *and* SETH,
and always to HELEN.

Contents

Acknowledgments

E VERY book is collaborative. At the very least, the past always fuses with the present. Burton Cooper edited this book with finesse and intelligence. My debt to him is great. Suzanne O'Connor typed endless drafts with equanimity, good humor, and that old Irish charm. Susan Westin and Greta Hendricks were always available for emergency alterations. Howard Zinn, Joseph Boskin, Edward Berger, and Andrew Morrison, all dear friends, criticized several chapters and, I believe, improved the argument.

None of us who studied with Louis Hartz can forget his brilliance and good fellowship. He trained us to look at America in a special and fruitful way.

Introduction

THE assassination of John Fitzgerald Kennedy in 1963 was the first of several shocks that precipitated a crisis of confidence in American society, an explosion of mistrust, a skepticism about fundamental values that continued into the early 1980s. For two decades public opinion pollsters reported that Americans were experiencing a profound loss of faith in politicians and parties, big business, labor leaders, the professions, and the judiciary. Millions of Americans believe that this crisis of confidence was precipitated by the baneful effects of self-interest and a corrosive and all-consuming materialism. The confidence gap extended to the core beliefs of the liberal tradition. The political alienation and anomie of the 1960s and 1970s were so pervasive that the American Dream, the mythic bedrock of the republic, was losing its magic. Some leading social scientists were concerned that a crisis of authority was a serious possibility.

This crisis of confidence was rooted in reality. The precipitous decline of national felicity was a response not merely to the president's assassination but also to the Vietnam War, the Watergate scandal, the Watts riots, student protests, the women's rights movement, the gay rights movement, the black rights movement, the emergence of new lifestyles and new sexual codes, the integration of public schools, affirmative action, and a proliferation of social welfare programs. These dislocations, threats, and annoyances were exacerbated by recurrent inflation, recession, and rising unemployment.

The 1960s and 1970s were turbulent decades, during which mistrusting America became a national pastime for rich and poor, black and white, educated and uneducated, Protestant, Catholic, Jew, Democrat, and Republican. The loss of confidence was bipartisan, multiracial, and ecumenical. This was a confidence gap of historic proportions in a nation where confidence and patriotism are the first assumptions of public life.

The United States is a culture of confidence, a nation whose self-esteem and aggressiveness were nourished by the conviction that it had discovered the self-evident truths of political economy—those natural and beneficent laws that produce social harmony and prosperity. Confidence in the republic was reinforced by a profound consciousness that, with its founding, the oppressions of Europe had been left behind, that America was a tabula rasa, capable of being molded into a prosperous and democratic society of equals. Self-evident truth became identified with free enterprise and electoral politics. Loyalty to the American way became a unanimous and compulsive reflex action, a petrified and dogmatic commitment that transcended the vicissitudes of the business cycle and political venality. Confidence became the national ethos; mistrust became aberrant and heretical. The decay of this positive public feeling, however, has been the leitmotif of recent decades.

Crises of confidence are rare and, therefore, revelatory, X-rays, as it were, that reveal the bones beneath the flesh of the body politic. When the bedrock of trust is eroded and the unanimity of the liberal tradition threatened, it is possible to explore the degree to which the American commitment is an artifact of nationalistic public relations, a false consciousness of massive proportions, or a genuine love of country. It is possible to locate, with some precision, what in the national terrain is anchored and what may give way in stormy seas.

Talk Radio and the American Dream is the first book to document and analyze a period of American history through tape recordings of hundreds of hours of talk radio. Talk radio is now a significant vehicle of public opinion in America. Thousands of shows in hundreds of cities accumulate a magnificent archive of Americana, an unparalleled oral history of our time. Thousands of hours of daily conversation, rich and prolix, serious and banal, largely working class, catalog the intimate concerns of daily life and comprise a record of political and social commentary that has never been tapped by students of American life. This massive and enormously rich record of the public sentiment is obliterated every few days when radio stations erase their tapes. Yet these tapes reveal the tension of American life: sorrow and anger, bigotry and tolerance, mistrust and pride in country. These tapes record a strong sense that public good and communal feeling are being eroded by the callous self-interest of big business and the venality of political apparatchiks.

This oral history, largely spontaneous and anonymous, is an astonishing testimony to the growing belief that something fundamental and corrosive is sapping the vitality of the republic. The diagnosis of callers is inchoate and diffuse, but the sense of malaise is there, particularly when callers articulate the petty concerns of daily life—the seemingly insignificant interchanges between neighbor and neighbor, customer and salesman, citizen and policeman. It is here that the callousness of the nation is exemplified in microcosm.

Talk radio is a particularly sensitive barometer of alienation because the hosts promote controversy and urge their constituencies to reveal the petty and grand humiliations dealt by the state, big business, and authority. Controversy and intimacy nourish the audience and multiply the station's revenues. But the unique quality of talk radio has much to do with the fact that it is the province of proletarian discontent, the only mass medium easily available to the underclass. The talk show is the most déclassé of media; it is the captive of smaller budgets, less-sophisticated technology, less-famous hosts, and relatively smaller audiences than television. Working men and women, the uneducated, and those who live on the margins of mainstream America need not fear the exposure that video creates. Anonymity reduces the reluctance of the uneducated. The abundant civic complaints that are a show's stock-in-trade nourish the urge to talk. As the prime conduit for proletarian despair, talk radio has become an oral history of the other America, a channel for the vast underground of discontent that lies below the calm surface of American life. As such, talk radio has become one of the very few delegitimizing voices of America. As a chronicle of disenchantment, the talk show represents the obverse of television's prime fairy tales: the Ewings and the Carringtons.

Talk Radio and the American Dream utilizes this goldmine of Americana to document the turbulent history of the 1960s and 1970s. Seven hundred hours of broadcasting on two of New England's most important political talk shows—one conservative, the other liberal—were tape-recorded in 1977 and 1982. The tapes were used to construct portraits that are more than impressionistic representations of the time but less than scientific abstractions of reality. Talk radio is not a random sample of public opinion, but it has a vibrancy and emotional range, a nakedness and reality that can never be conveyed by the quantitative measures of the public opinion pollster. This first effort to use talk radio for serious social analysis is frankly experimental, but the portrait of reality that emerges is unique, a stunning and poignant parade of American types.

Talk radio as oral history has advantages over survey research. Talk radio can be truly a human interchange, faceless but heartfelt, between real people, not pollsters and respondents playing roles and bound by rituals. During two or three hours of talk radio, it is possible to develop dialectic that reveals a complexity and a wide range of feelings. Talk radio is confrontational; it presents opinion responding to contradiction. In this sense it is richer than the static opinions frozen in time by the pollster.

The talk is full of anger towards the politicians and parties and towards big business and labor. The lower middle class and proletarian callers who often make radio their private preserve despise social welfare, affirmative action, and secular humanism. But they also attribute many of the nation's ills to unrestrained self-interest and excessive materialism. They speak of their alienation and powerlessness, of the futility of voting, and of the corruption and unresponsiveness of politicians. They sense the disappearance of communal bonds and the decline of mutual aid. They speak of the maldistribution of social justice. The crisis for them is moral, not merely political.

There is a brooding but inchoate feeling among callers that the moral basis of the nation has gone sour, a sense that the old ethical and moral guidelines are losing their force. There is a sense of despair—not concretized, but present—a sense that the American Dream is under seige. The deeper crisis is located in this despair. It is here that the talk captures the sadness as well as the anger of the age.

Talk radio is not merely a record of the past, it is a portent of things to come. The talk of working Democrats, violently opposed to the welfare state, full of hatred of the poor, blacks, and the counterculture, forecasted the Reagan triumph. Talk radio in the late 1970s was inundated by Democratic working men and women who were fed up with their party's commitment to economic equality. Mistrust of America converted Democrats into conservatives.

Talk Radio and the American Dream attempts to document this shift and the wave of powerlessness and alienation that swept the nation. The effort naturally leads to comment on the possibility that future crises of confidence may become crises of legitimacy, large-scale withdrawals of allegiance.

Chapter 1, "Mistrusting America," deals with the creation of a culture of confidence in America and the emergence of the crisis of confidence. Chapter 2, "Talk Radio and Proletarian Despair," explores the milieu of political talk radio: the role of the host, the guests, and the nature of the talk. Chapter 3, "Everything That's Good We No Longer Have," presents the angry talk of neoconservatives, which now reverberates in national politics. Chapter 4, "Have a Nice Day," is preoccupied with talk of the debasement of the manners and morals in daily life. Chapter 5, "I Looked in His Eyes and I Knew He Was a Crook," examines the politics of the alienated voter. Chapter 6, "To Catch a Thief," presents several strategies to counter the stereotype of the politician as liar and crook. The degradation of American politics is the issue. Chapter 7, "Liberal Language and the Failure of Class Consciousness," considers the impediments to class consciousness in America and some preconditions for a more radical politics. Finally, "Nagasaki Mon Amour," concerns the trust in America of one of the men who directed the atomic bomb run on Nagasaki.

TALK RADIO
AND THE
AMERICAN
DREAM

1

Mistrusting America

A PICTURESQUE version of American history, a fable, has become an article of national faith. The United States was settled by men and women who fled the oppressions of the Old World. The absence of these oppressions—monarchic absolutism, aristocratic privilege, and religious intolerance—made the Enlightenment dream of equality and democracy a reality in America. Americans in the eighteenth century, so the fable goes, were aware of their unique and good fortune. They had left the feudal world of Europe behind, and had escaped the burdens of the past: ritual, magic, tyranny, class, and superstition. Their prospects were unlimited. Land was abundant and easily accessible. Democracy was the natural heir to this shared opulence; God and nature seemed to assure a humane, prosperous, and democratic outcome. Confidence in America was the natural response to this bounty.

Trust in America was buoyed by the rhetoric of patriots, preachers, and burghers, who reminded their fellow expatriates of the profound difference between tyranical Europe and free America. This dichotomy was understood to be God's redemptive work.

The New World was cast in the image of the Garden of Eden, a wondrous and bountiful miracle created for man by God. This miraculous image and the reality of a rich and fruitful land promoted a culture of trust and optimism, a national sense that America offered the good life and could be trusted to fulfull its promise.

Americans luxuriated in this vision of a new and unprecedented age of freedom. The enormous natural advantages of the nation generated a dream of abundance and a belief that America could provide social justice. Optimism, trust, possibility, expansion, affluence, and confidence became the building blocks of the national psyche.

The uniqueness of America is symbolized by its revolution: the only upheaval designed to preserve the past rather than destroy it. The revolution was fought to preserve the ancient rights of Englishmen, little more. The American Revolution, like no other was quietly affirming and unprophetic. There is a very important cue here: A revolution that is so down to earth—so without prophets and visions—can occur only in an advantaged and self-confident nation. The French writer Alexis de Tocqueville understood these revolutionary origins: "The great advantage of the Americans is, that they have arrived at a state of democracy without having to endure a democratic revolution; and that they are born equal, instead of becoming so." With this blessing, America became a rock of ages.

The founding fathers mediated the theories of John Locke and based America on liberal self-evident truths: men are created equal and possess equal rights, sovereignty resides in the people, private property is sacrosanct. The belief that it embodied nature's universal truths made America a revered and sacred community—honored, trusted, destined to convert the faithless. With such a blessing, confidence can easily give way to hubris.

The rapid triumph of capitalism reinforced America's identification of moral superiority with free enterprise. The production and reproduction of affluence transformed laissez faire from an eighteenth-century novelty into a national religion. Capitalism became the American way. This fusion of moral rectitude with affluence defined the American experience and reaffirmed the image of America as a Garden of Eden, a "City upon a hill," a cornucopia of equality and prosperity, a unique experience in world history. This image of opportunity, plenty, and equality has been the popular and official conception of the republic since its founding. It is a confident and trusting image, frozen in our national monuments and our official art.

This commitment to America and free enterprise, however, is not relaxed. It is strident, dogmatic, and compulsive; it is passionate and metaphysical. Free enterprise has become a matter of such transcendant conviction that to test its reality is superfluous. The Great Depression, disastrous wars, and political scandals have not seriously disrupted the true believer nor created a demand for systemic diagnosis. Nourished by apparently self-evident norms, and thus beyond history, patriotism in America can easily give way to visceral super-patriotism.

Despite the forces that discourage dissent, despite the liberal orthodoxy that is our signature, America has developed a modest, basically polite, nonviolent tradition of dissent, a skepticism that is occasionally excited by gross inequality. Amercian critics and reformers speak in muted, nonradical tones. Neither the muckraking Progressives, nor the "radical" New Dealers systematically criticized the existing order or created a political party inimical to capitalism. With the exception of Populism, the constituency of mistrust never proposed a radical vision of a better society. Reformers have periodically focused attention on specific evils—bosses, political machines, trusts, corruption, collusive business practices—but they have not proposed remedies to alter the distribution of power of justice in fundamental ways. America, in the midst of its most cataclysmic depression, did not produce a master critic of the system, or a mass conservative or radical movement, or a prophetic visionary armed with a new model of production and a correlative social ethic. The genius of American politics has been its ability to pacify without sacrificing, to produce and reproduce, from generation to generation, an enormous reservoir of felicity and patriotism.

But a collapse of this magnanimous feeling occurred in the two decades preceding Ronald Reagan's election. An unprecedented nationwide explosion of mistrust, an erosion of faith in America, was precipitated by repeated shocks such as the Vietnam War, the Watergate scandal, ghetto riots, the women's rights movement, the gay rights movement, the racial equality movements, inflation, recession, and stagflation. The country often appeared to be out of control. During the 1960s and 1970s, much of the country lost confidence in the White House, the Congress, and the electoral process. Big business, many of the professions, and labor leaders also became suspect. Virtually every section of the country, every social class, and racial and religious group, experienced a precipitous falling away from traditional loyalties. There was an unprecedented crisis of confidence.

This crisis was characterized by a profound sense that the gap between the American Dream and reality had become intolerable. Large minorities questioned the virtue of self-interest as a way of life. Many began to doubt that a nation so divided could generate a sense of community to nourish the mutuality of interest and felicity that produces civic culture: compliance to law, willingness to accept defeat, a disposition to compromise. A widespread and prolonged withdrawal of trust threatened the civic order.

During the 1960s and 1970s, mistrust of America became the centerpiece of political culture. Pollsters reported that political alienation and feelings of powerlessness had reached unprecedented levels. A substantial majority of Americans believed that the distribution of social justice had become profoundly skewed.

The confidence gap was so public, the despair and anger so deep, that every public opinion pollster and survey research center—Gallup, Harris, Roper, Yankelovich, Caddell, Seasonwein, Cantril, the University of Michigan Center for Political Studies, the Opinion Research Corporation, the National Opinion Research Center, Cambridge Reports, ABC, CBS, *The New York Times*, and *The Washington Post*—documented the rising tide of mistrust, and raised questions concerning the viability of the American system. The loss of faith was so sudden and so dramatic that pollsters refer to it as an "explosion of mistrust," a crisis of confidence.

Mistrusting America became a national preoccupation for rich and poor, black and white, educated and uneducated, Protestant, Catholic, Jew, Democrat, and Republican. There were refinements, exceptions, and asymmetries within each group, but the thrust of national public opinion was clear: a confidence gap of historic proportions.

Daniel Yankelovich, one of the nation's most thoughtful pollsters, documented the crisis.

> We have seen a steady rise of mistrust in our national institutions. . . . Trust in government declined dramatically from almost 80% in the late 1950's to about 33% in 1976. Confidence in business fell from approximately a 70% level in the late '60s to about 15% today. Confidence in other institutions—the press, the military, the professions—doctors and lawyers—sharply delcined from the '60s to mid-70s. A two-thirds majority felt that what they think "really doesn't count." Approximately three out of five people feel the government suffers from a concentration of too much power in too few hands, and fewer than one out of five feel tht congressional leaders can be believed. One could go on and on. The change is simply massive. Within a ten-to-fifteen-year period, trust in institutions has plunged

down and down, from an almost consensual majority, two-thirds or more, to minority segments of the American public.[1]

These data are unprecedented in the history of survey research. The decline in trust was precipitous and all-inclusive. This explosion of mistrust matured within a few years, and became a contagious alienation that ultimately spread to the moral foundation of the nation: liberal ethics, the fundamental building block of legitimacy. The extent of bad feeling was so pervasive that some politicians and scholars speculated that a crisis of legitimacy was possible, a widespread withdrawal of allegiance. The crisis of confidence was, in essence, a bitter outcry that democratic routines and the system of social justice had been inverted.

By the late 1970s government, big business, and labor had lost substantially more than half the support they had enjoyed in the 1950s. In 1980, in the land of Horatio Alger, less than one-sixth of the people retained their confidence in big business. The working man's representatives at the bargaining table were also in disrepute. In two dozen polls taken between 1966 and 1981, the proportion of the population expressing a "great deal of confidence" in the leaders of organized labor fell from 22 percent to 12 percent. When Ronald Reagan was first elected president, almost 70 percent of Americans believed that "the government is run for the benefit of a few big interests."[2]

During the late 1950s almost four-fifths of the American public felt confident about the role of government. In 1976, the level of trust had declined to approximately 38 percent. In 1958, less than one of every four people believed that there were "quite a few crooks" in government; in 1979, almost one-half held that view. In 1958, 43 percent agreed that the government wasted a great deal of money. Twelve years later, seventy-eight percent concurred.

During the 1960s and 1970s numerous pollsters reported a sharp decline in political efficacy, the belief that voting counts, that politics is understandable, that people have some meaningful influence on political outcomes. The ultimate test of political efficacy is the conviction that one has some say about what the government does.

During the 1960s and 1970s dozens of pollsters asked, "Do you agree or disagree with the statement, voting is the only way that people like me can have any say about how the government runs things." In 1964, almost 75 percent agreed. When Ronald Reagan took office, 58 percent agreed. Between 1960 and 1980, the proportion who agreed that politics was too complicated to understand, increased 12 percent. In 1960, the year of John F. Kennedy's triumph, only 27 percent believed that they had little or no say in what government does. A decade later, 45 percent reported that they lacked influence over the government. When President Reagan took office, 39 percent agreed with the statement, "People like me don't have any say about what the government does," and 48 percent felt that politics was too complicated to understand.[3] Two decades after myth-makers crafted Camelot and the national mood was reaffirmed by so many Beautiful People, perhaps one-third of all Americans felt politically alienated.

In the two decades following John Kennedy's death, majorities perceived the government as increasingly unresponsive and bureaucratic. Large numbers of people lost much of their faith in the meaningfulness of elections. Between 1964 and 1980, the Center for Political Studies at the University of Michigan attempted to measure the perceived responsiveness of the government. "Over the years, how much attention do you feel the government pays to what people think when it decides what to do—a great deal, some, or not much?" The proportion who responded "a great deal" declined from 32 percent in 1964 to 8 percent in 1980.[4]

By the time President Reagan was inaugurated, fewer than one of every two Americans believed that government was responsive to public opinion. This decline in confidence was paralleled by growing mistrust of political parties and elections. Between 1964 and 1980, the proportion of respondents who believed strongly that parties "help to make the government pay attention to what peole think" decreased from 41 percent to 18 percent, while faith in elections as responsive vehicles declined from 65 to 51 percent.[5] By 1980, less than one-fifth of the respondents had a "good deal" of faith in the responsiveness of parties, congressmen, or "the government." This dramatic decline in trust was accompanied by a sharp decline in party affiliation.

Pollsters explored perceptions of the attentiveness of congressmen during these decades. The Center for Political Studies, for example, reported that during the crisis of confidence, the proportion who believed that their congressman paid "a good deal" of attention declined from 41 percent to 16 percent.[6] The belief in popular sovereignty had seriously been weakened. The state and its agencies were no longer perceived as fiduciary agents, but as unresponsive enclaves of self-interest. The public sensed a profound negation of good faith, an illegitimacy, an inversion of good order and right.

Fifteen years of political and economic upheavals eroded the traditional optimism of the American people. Patrick Caddell, President Carter's pollster, reported that Americans, in the late 1970s, were becoming increasingly pessimistic about their personal lives and skeptical about the future of the country. Pollsters reported for the first time that a majority of Americans believed the near future would be worse than the present.[7] This finding, unique in the history of survey research, indicates that mistrust of the system had become personalized: Americans actually expected the quality of their daily life to decline.

The crisis of confidence was not merely political. Confidence in big business fell from approximately 70 percent in the late 1960s to 15 percent in 1977. Substantial majorities perceived big business as venal and motivated solely by self-interest. Big business, for example, was perceived as the prime dispoiler of the environment. Although majorities expressed their appreciation of the technological achievements of American business year after year, they nevertheless rated business negatively in several critical areas. Big business was considered to be uninterested in containing increases in the cost of living. Business was also perceived as actively involved in planned obsolescence and inadequately motivated to produce new and better products.[8]

The public service role and ethical standards of business were the subject of numerous public opinion polls during the crisis. Yankelovich, for example, asked respondents for several years whether they agreed or disagreed with the statement: "Business tries to strike a fair balance between profits and the interest of the public." In 1968, 70 percent agreed. The figure plummeted to 33 percent in 1970, and then declined to 23 percent in 1980. As of 1981, less than one of every five Americans believed that big business was willing to curb its own interests on behalf of the public interest.[9] The Roper Organization discovered, during the crisis of confidence, that two-thirds of their sample doubted that business advertising was honest. Six out of ten doubted that business paid its fair share of taxes.

Almost 70 percent agreed that business and industry were "far too often" not honest with the public.

Soon after the Abscam scandal, the Roper Organization queried respondents on the degree to which they believed that congressmen, top businessmen, and labor leaders dealt in "bribes and payoffs in return for favors." A substantial majority believed that top business executives and union officials were as guilty, if not more so, as the congressmen involved in Abscam. Substantial majorities also believed that business, labor, and political leaders were intensely self-interested and frequently dishonest. Roper's respondents felt that business leaders, compared to labor and political leaders, were more competent and intelligent, but less socially responsible.[10]

The crisis of confidence was contagious and touched nearly every realm of American life. Yankelovich, one of the most sensitive pollsters, estimated that the politically alienated segment of America doubled during the 1960s and 1970s.[11] By the late 1970s, four out of five Americans believed that political leaders could not be trusted.[12] Mistrust spread from one institution to another as the catalog of unresolved problems mounted. Not one major American institution or profession improved its status during the mistrustful decades, and several of the most prestigious—the Supreme Court, the clergy, higher education, the military, and the medical profession, for example—lost much of the moral authority that the public had traditionally bestowed upon them. Not one profession or institution was consistently favored with a majority vote of "great confidence," and only two, medicine and the scientific community, received the blessing of at least 40 percent.

The confidence gap is anomolous: an explosion of mistrust, a criticism of cultural values in a traditionally confident culture. By the mid-1970s, public opinion pollsters began to ask what had caused the crisis. After fifteen years of escalating mistrust, survey researchers discovered that sizable minorities believed that selfishness and materialism had much to do with the moral dissipation that had provoked the crisis.

In July, 1979, the Columbia Broadcasting System and *The New York Times* found that 86 percent of a national sample agreed "that there is a moral and spiritual crisis, that is, a crisis of confidence in this country today." In 1979, the Roper Organization presented respondents with twelve possible causes of the crisis and asked them to note which they thought were "the major causes of our problems today." A majority of Roper's respondents cited: "Let down in moral values (56%), lack of good leadership (52%), permissiveness in the courts (51%), wrongdoing in government (51%), and selfishness, people not thinking of others (50%)." Forty one percent selected "too much emphasis on money and materialism."[14]

The Roper report and other data gathered during the 1960s and 1970s indicate that the crisis was not an ephemeral and petty fit, not a tentative withdrawal of trust from political, business, and labor leaders. Mistrust was not the sole, or even the major attribute of the crisis. People were saddened by the state of the union. They felt powerless, bitter, abused, bypassed, and cheated of their birthright—as if the proper relation of state to citizen were out of joint. The crisis was the expression of anger at grotesque impropriety, inversion, and illegitmacy—a sense of perversion of social justice, of the negation of popular sovereignty, of the signification of oligarchy and abuse.

The crisis of confidence extended beyond political performance to the underlying ethical and moral foundations of the nation. The issue was not the ineffectiveness of public policy but the destructive and antihuman effects of self-interest and materialism, the ethical bases and goals of liberal societies. Self-interest, the allegedly beneficent wellspring of public good, the classic American virtue, the Darwinian centerpiece of progress, was perceived by many as a prime cause of America's troubles, as an agent of greed and inequity, as a major cause of antisocial behavior.

After fifteen years of mistrust, the issue for a growing minority of Americans was no longer the trustworthiness or competence of politicians or businessmen, but the social worth of the current political and business ethic. The quality of life was becoming an issue, rather than quantity of goods. The shattering of communal bonds was becoming an issue, rather than the protection of private rights. The crisis was, in fact, exercise in heresy: widespread skepticism towards self-interest and materialism is not a part of conventional American rhetoric. The crisis was also a national group therapy, a massive catharsis, an outpouring of anger, frustration, soul searching, and projecton.

The crisis ultimately became a plebiscite on the issue of social justice. By the late 1970s large majorities were convinced that the system of social justice was failing. Yankelovich commented on the prevailing perceptions of social justice:

> Indicators of disaffection . . . show widespread feelings of resentment against social justice. Quite substantial majorities of the public ranging from 60 percent to 80 percent feel that there are cracks in the system of social justice as it operates today. People have come to feel that those who work hard and live by the rules are being neglected, shunted around, exploited, while those who flaunt the rules and thumb their noses at the social norms get all the breaks. A Democratic society that depends on its citizens for its consensual authority draws strength from an unwritten contract whereby those who conform to prevailing norms come to feel that conformity pays off, while those who choose not to conform know that there is a price to bear for nonconformity. . . . We now have a situation where more than four out of five of our citizens seem to feel that the unwritten contract is not working properly, that the rewards of society go to those who fail to conform while those who do conform are made to feel like fools for faithfully observing the rules of the game.[15]

The crisis of confidence was a period of anger and reappraisal, a period when some of the customary clichés of legitimation were rejected or modified. Numerous public opinion surveys, for example, revealed that large majorities believed that "the rich get richer and the poor get poorer," and that the state is infused with oligarchy. Pollsters reported that large numbers of people no longer believed elections were meaningful instruments of popular sovereignty and no longer believed the state took its fiduciary obligation seriously. The dichotomy between power and powerlessness became the fulcrum of public opinion. Popular consciousness was becoming more sophisticated, more complex, more discriminating, and more alienated.

Notes

1. Daniel Yankelovich, "Emerging Ethical Norms in Public and Private Life" (unpublished manuscript), University Seminar, Columbia University, April 20, 1977. Quoted in Lipset & Schneider, p. 15.
2. Warren E. Miller, Arthur H. Miller, and Edward J. Schneider, *American Electoral Studies Data Sourcebook, 1952–1978* (Cambridge, Mass.: Harvard University Press, 1980), p. 257–259.

3. Seymour M. Lipset and William Schneider, *The Confidence Gap: Business, Labor & Government in the Public Mind.* Studies of the Modern Corporation (New York: The Free Press, 1983), p. 21.
4. Center for Political Studies, University of Michigan, 1980 American National Election Study (Wane C-3) quoted in Lipset & Schneider, p. 17.
5. Lipset & Schneider, p. 17.
6. Center for Political Studies, University of Micigan, 1980 American National Election Study (Wane C-3).
7. Patrick Caddell, "Crisis of Confidence I: Trapped in the Downward Spiral," *Public Opinion* 2 (Oct.-Nov. 1979).
8. Lipset & Schneider, pp. 29-32.
9. Yankelovich, Skelly, and White, Inc., "Trend of Anti-Business Sentiment 1968-81," cited in Lipset & Schneider, p. 183.
10. Roper Reports (New York: Roper Organization) November–December, 1980.
11. Yankelovich, ibid.
12. David Gergen, "A Report from the Editors on the Crisis of Confidence," *Public Opinion* 2 (Aug.-Sept. 1979), p. 2.
13. Confidence in Institutions, 1975-81, Opinion Research Corporation, 1975-81, quoted in Lipset & Schneider, p. 60.
14. Roper Reports 79-3 (New York: Roper Organization), Feb. 24, 1979.
15. Daniel Yankelovich, "The Status of Resentiment in America," *Social Research* 42 (Winter 1985), p. 763.

2

Talk Radio and
Proletarian Despair

A MERICA'S most distinguished public opinion pollsters documented the confidence gap for two decades. Hundreds of surveys produced thousands of bits of data. The pollsters quantified the crisis; provided detailed information concerning the distribution and intensity of mistrust among and between classes, socioeconomic groups, and races; and theorized on the meaning of the crisis. The most advanced apparatus of modern social science was used to interpret and reinterpret the data. The results are rich. The dimensions of mistrust in the 1960s and 1970s are clear.

The data are indispensable, but they are one step removed from the vibrancy of daily life: a flattened and abstracted representation of reality. Survey research quantifies public opinion, but it does not supply the affect, the conviction, and the anger. One may express confidence or mistrust with the deepest conviction, or in a half-hearted and tentative manner; the quantification of both expressions is the same. The crisis of confidence can be reduced to quantifiable measures, but it is really a conglomeration of hope, despair, anger, and disgust. Mistrust may be the expresson of rational calculation or intuitive reaction; each achieves its own political effect. But the depth of feeling, the nuance that ultimately defines reality, is not easily amenable to the pollsters' protocols.

Survey data, however, are not the only source available for analysis of the crisis. During the 1960s and 1970s, hundreds, if not thousands, of radio talk shows were aired, many of which featured public affairs. The crisis of confidence was a significant topic throughout the country. Alienated callers, in huge numbers, bombarded the airways with a calendar of estrangements—petty and grand. The agenda of talk radio during those decades featured the Vietnam War, the Watergate scandal, busing, black rioting, women's rights, gay rights, the failures of foreign policy, student uprisings, corruption in government, alternative lifestyles, inflation, recession, drugs, political efficacy—the gamut of public concern. This enormous mass of talk, from every section of the country, from every social group, comprises a rich archive of Americana, an opulent catalog of the complaints and mistrust that made up the crisis of confidence.

Talk radio is a primary source on the crisis. It presents the verbatim record of many who mistrusted big business and government, decried public corruption, and lost faith in labor leaders and the professions. Talk radio documents the feelings that lie behind the statistics. The verbatim record has a poignancy, a primordial quality, a dimensionality so rich that "live" protraits of the alienated may be drawn, sketches that capture the nuances of mistrust.

Many radio talk shows do not deal with public affairs. They cultivate audiences by purveying salvation, or sexual fulfillment, or Hollywood gossip, or the road to riches in real estate. They may be a barometer of popular culture, a calendar of bourgeois aspiration, but our concern here is with the escalation of political alienation and mistrust.

For three months in 1977, at a peak in the crisis of confidence, two of New England's most prominent political talk shows—one liberal, one conservative — were tape recorded. Both shows, broadcasting from Boston, were recorded again for three months in 1982. Approximately 700 hours of talk radio were recorded and analyzed, over a period of two years. Callers to radio talk shows do not constitute a random sample of the population. Greater Boston, with its long history of political corruption, may even be more mistrustful than most American cities. Scientific generalizations about public opinion based on callers to talk shows, regardless of the huge numbers involved, are not possible. Our purpose, however, is not quantification, but the construction of ideal or pure types: portraits of alienated Americans that illuminate the most common varieties of mistrust. Our task is to construct verbatim autobiography—that is, oral history. If the host is not intrusive, talk radio may be unedited oral history; it may also be contrived and censored by the host's need to direct and intrude. Talk radio is, in many ways, a more complete record of the crisis of confidence than survey data because much of the talk concerns mistrust of politics at the state and local level and the distress of everyday life—areas untouched by the pollsters.

Talk radio has become a window on the world for millions. Thousands of talk shows in hundreds of cities from early morning to late at night, day after day, month after month, deluge the airways with millions of words, expressing news, commentary, gossip, political propaganda, personal advice, scandal, debate on public issues, financial tips, and endless trivia. Guests abound: senators, congressmen, political candidates, chefs, clergy, columnists, celebrities, muckrakers, mystics, military men, scientists, financial tipsters, futurologists, environmentalists, men and women of letters, and crackpots. The talk show is psychiatrist, physician, guide to the perplexed, financial consultant, political adviser, sex therapist, clergyman, and cosmetician. Solicitude, entertainment, and advice are common coin: how to make a million in real estate, how to rear children, how to resolve sexual problems, how to achieve inner peace, how to lose weight, how to vote, how to transcend loneliness.

Talk radio is an archive of Americana. It is heir apparent to the tradition of self-improvement of which Horatio Alger and Dale Carnegie were masters. Talk radio dispenses the social gospel while attending to the gossipy world of Walter Winchell. It fuses pragmatism with magic, supplying secret formulas that will make a beauty of a beast or a millionaire of a pauper. The magic is supplied by the dietician, the sex therapist, or the clergyman. The talk show is a soul saver. It supplies a bit of Freud to salve the ego. It parades a millionaire up from the slums to reassure the poor but worthy. So much aid and comfort, so much controversy, so many opportunities to participate and identify, to love and hate, have made talk radio a unique growth industry that spawns addicts, entertains millions, and attracts large shares of advertising revenue.

Talk radio has its captive audience: the commuter, the parent tending child, the unemployed, the house-bound, and the insomniac. The audience ebbs and flows with "drivetime," the commute to and from work. Talk radio, led by a host sensitive to the value of open exchange, can be a remarkably democratic medium. The lines are open to all: few callers are screened; nondiscrimination is the policy. There is no color line, no political test, no registration, no qualification, no revelation of income or class, and no charge for access. The callers are protected by their anonymity.

The democratic potential of talk radio is enhanced by the fact that it is a déclassé enterprise compared to the other media. Talk radio has significantly lower budgets than television, smaller salaries and audiences, lower advertising revenues, less sophisticated equipment, and a more limited broadcasting range. Talk radio is the poor relation of the media, but it is the most participatory. The spontaneity and informality of talk radio free it of the restraints imposed by television's structured panel of experts, where established guests are expected to deserve the protocol of propriety, and where time is limited. Many talk shows broadcast for two or three hours several days a week. There is sufficient time to develop serious talk and rejoinder.

Talk radio attracts a substantial lower middle class and proletarian audience, which greatly affects the agenda of the shows and the nature of the discourse. Working-class listeners are often encouraged to participate by the host, who assumes that their natural estrangement will provoke a barrage of civic complaints and expressions of mistrust from others. Working men and women may be emboldened to participate by the absence of video, which relieves them of the shame that bourgeois society imposes on the unfashionable and less well educated. Talk radio is the only medium that often provides an audience for working-class sentiment. And it is the only medium not dominated by established figures, romance, cops and robbers, or celebrities.

This working-class audience is preoccupied with the idea that America is increasingly unresponsive to its needs and weak in its commitment to social justice. The loss of political power is a common theme. The harshness and dangers of urban life are a common civic complaint. Callers are concerned with the debasement of daily life, the decay of manners and morals, the incivility of social exchanges. They cite the failure of coworkers to say good morning or thank you, the failure to return a cafeteria tray, or their children's lack of respect for school and parents. They decry the sale of drugs in the local high school and the refusal to attend church. They are afraid to walk in their neighborhoods after dark, and they do not believe the police can be trusted. Like Tocqueville, they see the essence of culture in its daily habits, in the most commonplace exchanges.

These exchanges, between salesman and customer, driver and driver, politician and constituent, contain and symbolize the essential social and political content of the culture. Talk radio, at its best, poignantly reveals the crisis of confidence through discussion of these relationships.

Talk radio, however, is often trivial and boring. Three or four hours is a long time to sustain exciting conversation. A show is no better than the host and its callers; and there is no reason to believe that the witless will engage the host less frequently than the imaginative. The host is often unable to promote the talk he wants. The show then falls victim to petty complaints and personal anecdotes that apparently interest no one. The topic may be garbage collection, poor street lighting, or the lack of cable television—an excruciating calendar of obscure gripes. The truly professional host saves the program by relating this agenda to wider concerns: the distribution of social justice between rich and poor, for example.

Talk radio is potentially democratic and it can be a real forum, but it can also be an autocratic vehicle contrived by the host for the advancement of his ideological stock-in-trade or favored candidate. The host is a professional talker and manipulator; dialectic and argumentation are his forté. The callers, with rare exceptions, are unable to match his skill. Many are nervous, not sure of precisely what they have in mind, and even less sure of how to express it. Many find argumentation intimidating. The situation is inherently one-sided. The host can terminate calls; the producer may screen them; a clever and forceful host can easily dominate the show.

Political talk radio is structured by the ideology of the host. His political philosophy and moral disposition determine the agenda, channel the ebb and flow of talk, and motivate some to call more than others. Freedom of speech can be instantly abridged with the flick of a switch. The host provokes, soothes, encourages, condemns, forecloses options, and oten avoids equal time. His style and world view can promote a real interchange or create the illusion of one.

The talk show has its own theatrics. The host becomes adept at the "put down," the screaming epithet, the dramatic onslaught, or the seduction. He becomes a master of the verbal martial arts. He knows the most dramatic moment to liquidate his adversary. He baits the caller and provokes extremist or simple-minded arguments—a racist tirade or an antisemitic remark. He becomes strident, defames the caller, assumes a dignified posture, introduces some reason, and then demolishes his victim. He, and no one else, can choose between democracy and freedom of speech or thought control. The caller, however, has little reason to hide his true feelings. He is anonymous and unseen, beyond retribution, although a potential target of the host's invective.

The host has more reason to adopt a mask than the caller because he is in the entertainment and advertising business. He is a pitchman, and a poseur, always sensitive to the show's ratings and commercial appeal. He must prod and promote, excite and involve his listeners. He often does this by creating a political melodrama, replete with heroes, knaves, fools, and conspirators. American history, particularly contemporary history, becomes a morality play, a cataclysmic struggle between good and evil—for conservative and liberal hosts alike. For the conservative host, the Protestant ethic and the spirit of capitalism, the true America, has been despoiled by inept and meddlesome pseudosocialists parading as Democrats. The liberal dramaturgy centers around an oligarchical and corrupt America that pacifies its poor while reproducing them, generation after generation, for corporate exploitation. Both types of talk show excite different but overlapping sets of alienated voters, those who feel bypassed and discriminated against by the social welfare state, and those who feel politically powerless in the face of corrupt and oligarchical political elites.

These melodramas contain little that is muted or gray. There is only good or evil, a dichotomous world in which the wise and moral choice is clear. The scenario offers a guide for the perplexed. The clarity of the moral choices resolves doubt. The fusion of myth and history provides the audience with boundless opportunities to verify their own values. There is a biblical quality to these morality plays: a fall from grace, redemption, devils and angels, and the true faith.

Much of the talk is affected by the melodrama and much of the audience is preselected by its appeal. The scenario sets the agenda, segments the audience, provides psychological rewards and punishments for callers, establishes a frame of reference, offers moral enlightenment, infuses fact with value, and enhances both alienation and hope. The host builds his audience, the radio station's advertising revenues, and his own salary by tailoring the drama to the daily news and the callers' prejudices. He must make the show controversial and entertaining. Conservative and liberal hosts cannot permit insipid talk to run on too long; they must, therefore, banish fools and bores or use them as foils. The adept host does exactly this. He becomes an agent provocateur, an antagonist who excites Bible-thumpers, ideologues, antisemites, and super-patriots to greater extremes in an effort to elicit their deepest prejudices. He then denudes the true believer; exposes false logic, fallacy, and prejudice through satire and invective; and retires to invite public accolade.

The gambit usually produces a barrage of invective. The aggressive host escalates the combat and orchestrates the attack, bearing in mind the dangers of libel law, the constraints of the Federal Communications Commission, and the sensibility of his public to aggression. The talk show is not a vehicle of unadulterated free speech, but of orchestrated free speech—a fusion, as it were, of provocation, censorship, and self-expression.

The shows achieve a contrived authenticity, in which speech is both spontaneous and crafted. The host quotes an inflammatory article: the Reagan administration designates ketchup as a vegetable for purposes of school lunch programs, or the Department of Defense pays $500 for a hammer. He seeks outrage and usually gets it. He provokes a discussion through contrivance, but the talk that ensues may mature if host or caller relates the issue—even an absurd issue—to more national concerns. The subject of ketchup and school lunches, for example, led to a discussion of the class bias of the Reagan administration and to an exchange on whether electoral politics offers a meaningful remedy to the poor. One sophisticated caller spoke of the maldistribution of nutrition among classes and the use of food as an instrument of national and international policy. The $500 hammer naturally became a dual cause célèbre: the basis for a conservative attack on bureaucracy and a liberal critique of bloated defense budgets.

The gap between the American Dream and reality is a frequent topic. The alienation and anger of the working class is documented daily with stories of unemployment and unequal opportunity, shabby living conditions, inadequate police protection, the burdens of high taxes, and the pampering of welfare recipients. The liturgy is not unusual; but the presentation by the abused on radio, heard by tens of thousands, is unusual. No mass medium in America is as available to the disenchanted as talk radio, none is so prone to undermine the legitimacy of America or so eager to transmit the pathos of powerlessness.

The delegitimizing quality of political talk radio stems, in part, from the fact that alienated callers often frame political issues in terms of class and equity. The issue is power, powerlessness, and the abuse of power. Oligarchy, governance by the rich, and widespread political corruption are the common complaints. Elections are perceived as purchasable by campaign contributors and meaningless to voters. The interest of the alienated is in who prospers and who is pauperized, who manipulates and who is manipulated, who is morally delinquent, who is morally observant. These dichotomies are very real to callers, who perceive politics and economics as a struggle for scarce resources, a contest in which the triumph of the rich necessitates the debilitation of the poor. Daily life is not usually portrayed as a random occurrence, or an act of God, or the unholding of democratic and egalitarian forces; rather, it is described with anger and sadness as an unfair struggle in which inequality of resources predetermines the distribution of justice and comfort. There is less talk of the American Dream than of powerlessness and inevitability. Talk radio has calls from patriotic advocates of the view that opportunities still abound in the land of the free, but this is not the leitmotif of talk radio. The message is largely countercultural and "un-American," a role that sets talk radio apart from its more conformist brethren in the media.

In 1982, five years after the first set of radio talk shows were taped, most callers continued to talk of a nation in serious trouble, a nation infused with some moral and spiritual malaise. Despite the apparent resurgence of patriotism that Mr. Reagan facilitated, the talk is vigorously antipolitical. Politics remains a dead-end: unresponsive and corrupt, unable to cleanse the environment, unable and unwilling to revivify urban life, unable to curb crime, unable to curb the arms race. The talk is of the failure of the church, the family, the police, and the schools to maintain moral standards. The talk is angry. Insiders of all kinds manipulate, prosper, and benefit by tax loopholes, but perform little or no useful function. It is clear from hundreds of hours of talk, tutored and untutored, that a reserve army of the discontented exists.

Radio talk leaves the impression that traditional liberal and conservative perspectives are increasingly uncongenial to the callers.

Callers have little or no sense of what the nation might do to stop the malaise, other than spend less, reduce support for the underclass, and arm more vigorously. The contradiction goes unattended.

Talk radio leaves an impression of widespread distress, an impression of a stalemate, a sense that America contains a political vacuum that may be a precurser to something new and dramatic. Callers provide a hint of what is to come. Their alienation has led them to focus less on economic and political matters and more on the question of what constitutes a good Christian life. Moral and ethical issues have become increasingly relevant to callers. They are preoccupied with the decline of the Protestant ethic and the role of state in promoting parisitism among welfare recipients and in inhibiting self-reliance. They are discouraged by the permissiveness of the courts, the destruction of the schools, the ease of obtaining abortions, and the debilitating effects of affirmative action. As America becomes increasingly materialistic, its politics become more infused with fundamentalist moralism.

These tensions are evident in political talk radio. Callers are divided between those with a commitment to the more traditional and morally infused ethos of the nineteenth centry—an ethos that elevates the family, religion, piety, and work, and rewards sexual repression—and those with a modernist outlook that emphasizes liberalizing social and sexual relations and state aid to the underclass. The conflict portends a more uncompromising political stance: one that is infused with moral righteousness and that offers a choice between unmitigated good and evil—the right to life, as it were, or murder.

The presentation of this conflict on talk radio has a delegitimizing effect. The other mass media, however, are inherently socializing agencies, conduits of middle-class morality that reaffirm consumerism and legitimize free enterprise and existing political practice. They reinforce the American Dream and provide ideals for bourgeois aspiration like the Ewings and the Carringtons of *Dallas* and *Dynasty*. The advertising that supports television is basically an invitation to adornment and conspicuous consumption. Political talk radio, however, often contrasts the sordidness of daily life with the official image of how life is lived in America.

The subversive effect of talk radio is often strengthened by guests, the crown jewels of talk radio, who energize and authenticate the show as entertainment and education. The importance of the guest celebrity reflects the host's prestige and enlarges it. The array of guests we recorded during 700 hours of talk radio was extraordinary: Secretary of the Interior James Watt; Ralph Nader; Eldridge Cleaver; the Imperial Wizard of the Ku Klux Klan; Hermann Kahn; Dr. Helen Caldicott; senators Paul Tsongas, Edward Kennedy, Robert Dole, Barry Goldwater; Admiral Elmo Zumwalt; Michael Harrington; Victor Laski; representatives Gerry Studds and Barney Frank; civil libertarian Alan Dershowitz; Speaker of the House Tip O'Neill; Majority Leader James Wright; Abbie Hoffman; Helen Gurley Brown; Jack Anderson; Pete Hammill; the theologian Harvey Cox; and Charles Schultz, the creator of Snoopy. The assistant director of the U.S. Arms Control and Disarmament Agency also appeared, as well as the director of the Council on Foreign Relations, the president of the U.S. Chamber of Commerce, the chairman of the American Civil Liberties Union, the television critic of *The New York Times*, the chairman of the Gay Task Force, dozens of authors in search of sales, and numerous foreign correspondents, scientists, and economists.

These guests bring an enormous range of knowledge and opinion to talk radio; much of it is instrumental, much is political, and most is contemporary. The calendar for three months included discussions of the rights of nonsmokers and gays, the causes of homosexuality, the right to life, the reliability of air traffic controllers, the advantages of credit unions, the wisdom of busing, the inequities of affirmative action, the security of banks, the efficacy of supply-side economics, the constitutionality of school prayer, the inequities of social welfare, how to prevent child abuse, how not to be cheated by auto body shops, how to make a million dollars, how to lose weight, how to control pornography, how to stay out of the hospital, how to find God, the balance of payments, how to buy insurance, the rights of the American Nazi Party, the efficacy of a nuclear freeze, the federal deficit, and—the sine qua non of bourgeois talk radio—how to buy real estate without a down payment.

The expertise and controversiality of the guests often generate a richly discursive and interactive response. One topic leads to another, fresh opinion is interjected, argument is provoked, dialectic ensues. A textured and prolix public record accumulates, the product of challenge and response. So many issues are raised over such a long period that one can discern continuities and structures of thought, uncertainties and contradictions. There is a metaphoric quality to the talk; the sudden shifts of affect and innuendo are full of meaning but difficult to quantify.

Talk radio, as we have noted, is enriched by the large amount of time available for point and counterpoint, which generates a reflexive, evolving opinion not avalable in the structured protocol of the pollster. Because talk shows air daily, it is possible to sense quick and spontaneous shifts in public opinion, to record immediate responses to significant events, and to hear reactions unmediated by the time and memory.

The revelatory quality of talk radio and its capacity to expose, however, are muted by the fact that the talk show, like the news on television and radio, often trivializes significant issues and treats the mundane as if it is transcendantly important. Discussions of nuclear survival are often preceded and followed by guests who ask whether one can trust banks or auto body shops. The sublime and the ridiculous receive equal time, and often evoke equally contentious disputes. A discussion of the Holocaust may last no longer than the guest's plane schedule permits. Although the host often defers to a celebrated guest, he tends to treat all issues with equal gravity. He is a pitchman who sells advertising, and must therefore maximize the dramatic power of each moment. By democratizing and emotionalizing all issues, he elevates the trivial and trivializes the significant. This trivialization is reinforced when discussion of significant issues is truncated by commercial interruptions.

There is a potential conflict between the commercial obligations of the media and their ability to be serious. Even talk shows that cater to a politically sophisticated audience cannot survive on a steady diet of guests like Hermann Kahn or Ralph Nader. Hosts operate on the assumption that there is a limit to the amount of sad and serious talk that audiences are willing to absorb. Talk radio is, above all else, entertainment, so the guest list includes rock stars, masters of haute cuisine, Wall Street wizards, and celebrities from Broadway, Hollywood, and Las Vegas.

The wide range of topics and the disputatiousness of the host and guests provide the audience with much opportunity to love and hate, join a common cause, voice a grievance, identify, project, aspire, talk, and be heard. The guest may be perceived as the devil's disciple, a miracle worker, a psychotherapist, or a moral delinquent. This opportunity to cathect is what commits listeners to the host and builds an audience.

On Monday the talk show may provide an ombudsman, a spiritual adviser, or someone complaining about crime. On Tuesday a sex therapist or a guide to the perplexed may be featured. Wednesday provides an optimistic double bill: a way out of the arms race and a list of the best automobile mechanics in town. The host, like the preacher, caters to many constituencies. The preachment and the pitch ultimately depend upon a suffering clientele with a will to believe. The show succeeds when this will is tapped and the talk resonates with some real fear or hope. The great host creates this resonance. Like the great therapist, the host forges a personal bond and lets the transference complete the process.

The guest, in many different ways, helps to create this resonance. The guest as magician and purveyor of glad tidings, for example, is a favorite. The salesman of the transcendent may show the way to God, or the path to quick weight loss, or the arcane manipulations that guarantee a fortune overnight. There is always a key, a secret, a simple trick, a golden rule, a magical way to obviate the barriers and pain of existence. The guest makes it clear that success is a matter of will. Talk radio feeds the desire for instant gratification. It succeeds in appealing to one part of its audience by affirming the value of positive thinking and the American Dream, and to another part by delegitimizing that dream. One guest extolls the virtues of private enterprise while another excoriates multinational corporations. Talk radio portrays a Hobbesian America of unmitigated self-interest and a Whitmanesque land of milk and honey.

The positive thinking and wizardry of the magicians is counter-balanced by the gravity of guests who specialize in nuclear strategy and disarmament. Global survival has become a standard topic for talk radio, not merely because it is a crucial issue of public discourse, but because it excites listeners. Hermann Kahn and Helen Caldicott offer the audience an opportunity not merely to think and reflect for an hour, but a chance to cathect with Armageddon. They elevate the talk show to the level of the academy.

Glad tidings restore the balance. The host produces boosters, patriots, travel agents, and do-gooders who affirm life's possibilities and praise America the beautiful. They remind the audience of the golden age—Babe Ruth, Lou Gehrig, and Rudolph Valentino. They preach the virtues of American know-how, reaffirm the value of elections, and testify to the presence of equal opportunity. They describe the scenic beauty of Santa Fe and the Grand Canyon. They cite themseves as proof that the Horatio Alger hero lives. And they thank American people for their contributions to research on muscular distrophy or the Jimmy Fund. Their nostalgia, their success, their good deeds, and their very presence testify to the virtues of the American way. They make people feel good, and they legitimize the nation. They counterbalance the purveyors of cynicism and insure the parity of opinion that creates an illusion of impartiality.

These loyal and successful practitioners of bourgeois virtue stand in sharp contrast to another group of guests whose lifestyles are exotic and shocking. The Imperial Wizard of the Ku Klux Klan, the professor who advocates the genetic inferiority of blacks, and the communist, join the homosexual, the transvestite, the exconvict, the Russophile, the prostitute, and the pimp to scandalize, anger, and titillate middle-class sensibility. Talk radio prospers because it creates something resembling an all-or-nothing situation in which listeners are "forced" to endure some dissonance in exchange for every bit of affirmation that they receive. The dissonance may turn them away, but the affirmation forces their return.

The deviant guest soon gives way to the salesman who caters to the bourgeois hunger for good food, good taste, and good gossip. Practitioners of haute cuisine reveal the secret of a great souffle. Inside dopesters unveil the mysteries of celebrities and the peccadilloes of the Washington establishment. The progeny of Amy Vanderbilt enlighten the nouveau riche on the correct use of forks and spoons. Talk radio is wish fulfillment and dream, a glimpse of the good life.

But talk radio can also be a model of mutual aid and a primer in the art of problem-solving. Every day one or two callers ask for aid and comfort—a nursing mother seeks advice on how to make her husband more cooperative, an unemployed shipworker needs employment, a son wants a proper nursing home for his mother, a grieving daughter needs to know how to live and smile again, a young intern who has just lost his first patient wonders whether he can continue to practice medicine. The response is heart-warming. Practical advice and moral succor are supplied to the needy: everything from the names of potential employers to agencies to talk to about the inevitability and mystery of death. Talk radio, in this posture, is enormously reaffirming. The number of people who wish to help is large, and their reservoir of good will seems unbounded. It is here that one senses the existence of a true community,— of a bonding that transcends self-interest. It causes one to wonder why such goodness has not become a model for social relations in general.

The talk show is not merely engaged in problem-solving and mutual aid, it is also a unique educational establishment for the masses, a relaxed and permissive center of learning, with open enrollment. There are no requirements and no examinations, but there are visiting "fellows" available for briefings and tutorials—scholars whose work is customarily available only in university bookstores or libraries. Many of the "faculty" have published. Some are articulate and much in demand by the students; others are boring and attract only limited enrollment. There may be class discussion and, occasionally, as in the university, fruitful exchange.

But this educational process is fragile. The host can terminate class at any time, alter the curriculum, deny tenure, or invite third-rate lecturers. The college lacks an integrated curriculum, and the courses are brief. The lectures may be unfocused, and the students are frequently unable to pursue the issues. The dean may transform a lecture into a morality play or refuse to pursue subtleties if he believes that it is in the interest of higher enrollments.

The analogy should not be over-drawn, but the fact remains that talk radio can expose large numbers of people to serious talk—people who might otherwise be committed mostly to candlepin bowling. Despite the primitive quality of the learning experience, thousands of hours are made available for people to share expertise and opinion, answer questions, cite bibliography, and debate callers. This is a unique American institution—a remarkable gift to those unwilling or unable to read.

The obstacles to open discussion are substantial. Political talk radio, however, is now established, and attracts large audiences. It is also one of the very few institution that serve as a proletarian outlet. It is the only medium that frequently encourages the reserve army of the poor and alienated to articulate their mistrust. Political talk radio is a wonderful archive of the crisis of confidence.

3

Everything That's Good
We No Longer Have

POLITICAL talk radio is a barometer of political discontent, a
harbinger of political change. The radio talk shows of 1977 leave
no doubt that the Democratic Party was in disarray, no doubt that
an enormous constituency of angry Democratic working men and
women were waiting for an alternative to forced busing, affirmative
action, and social welfare. The voices of talk radio spoke of the
powerlessness of the people and the power and corruption of the
state and big business. The drive for equality had convinced callers
that there was something drastically wrong with the dispensation of
social justice.

The overreaching theme was mistrust: mistrust of oligarchy, mistrust of permissiveness, mistrust of secular humanism in the schools,
mistrust of state action to buttress the underclass. Talk was also
preoccupied with emasculation: powerlessness to achieve meaningful
political outcomes through elections, powerlessness to combat political corruption, powerlessness to rescue the Protestant ethic and
individualism. The callers were angry, bitter, vengeful, and ripe for
a conservative patriotic revival. They sought the restoration of three
principles upon which the republic was founded: individualism, self-
reliance, and minimal government intervention. The crisis of confidence was the bedrock upon which Reaganism was built, the most
visible sign that Democratic social policy had run its course.

Seven callers, typical of the thousands we recorded, voice their
mistrust of America:

I can't put my finger on it. I don't know exactly what is wrong. But something is very wrong with this country. Something has happened. And it is rotten. Young girls in high school are pregnant. People in parks get raped. Criminals, who are obviously guilty, are saved by all kinds of technicalities, all kinds of clever lawyers. And they go out and steal again. You know what I mean? And the judges, liberal judges, seem more interested in giving people their rights than doing justice. The two are not the same, you know. But that's not all. I am afraid to go out at night and so are most of my friends. So we sit at home and lock our doors. What's wrong? No wonder there's so much trouble with kids. Watch television all day—cops, robbers, murders, drugs, filth—not much else—cops, robbers, murders, drug busts. What do we expect kids to do when this filth is on everyday?

Everybody wants everything and they want it now. Greed, that's what it's about—greed. And it doesn't seem to make much difference how they get it. It's okay to break the rules. It's okay to steal and cheat—look at the legislature, look at Boston. Look at all the business scandals. The old rules are gone. The old ways of doing things are dead. People laugh at the idea of a day's pay for a day's work. Today, the idea is to cheat the boss as much as possible. People laugh at people who work hard for regular pay and admire and hate people who make big money manipulating stocks. The less you help society, the more you make. And the reverse is true. Teachers, nurses, what they get paid. We trust our kids with them, but we won't pay them. It's crazy and it's going to ruin us.

Government provides the message that it pays not to work. Forget being a producer. Just join the ranks of the parasites. It's an immoral thing to do, to just sit back and let someone else work for you, especially when that someone is being forced to do it. . . . The system encourages people to be immoral. In fact, it makes it difficult for people to not be immoral. . . . Because your father works he is being penalized. Does that make any sense? You can live with yourself if you work . . . you're not beholden to anybody else . . . you earn your own way.

Where is the church? Empty. What are the schools doing? What hapened to families? People don't seem to care anymore. I'm not smart enough to explain what's happened, although I'm sure it's connected to the idea that it's okay to be as selfish as you want and it's okay to want everything. People really feel this way. It's right under your nose. There's been a big change. And it's all rotten. You know I'm right.

Everybody talks about why the country produced Watergate and why defense contractors rob the government, and corporations don't give a damn about our rivers and streams. Everybody knows the answer but they don't want to talk about it. It makes America look rotten. The holy buck, that's why money, money . . . who cares about your neighbor or the consumer? America is the buck. Everyone is on the make, and why not, schoolteachers, parents, magazines . . . everyone, everywhere says this is the American way, the American Dream, and it's a good way because from selfish—is supposed to come public good. You know the old capitalist saw, self-interest ultimately serves everyone. The cheapest product at the best price and all that stuff. Let's face it, we know it's a bunch of——! Nobody believes any more that what's good for General Motors is good for America. What a laugh!

Selfishness is killing America. It's a sickness and it's anti-Christian. When everyone is on the make, and few are restrained, we know what happens—the powerful get richer and the weak are more exploited. Look at what's happened under Reagan. It makes people look cheap and nasty. It makes the poor feel like victims. It corrupts friendship. I am no socialist, but I know this is killing us. It makes people hostile and wary. Everyone is worried about being cheated and there is little feeling that we have much in common. There isn't any general welfare. What does the dollar say—many in one. That's a myth, isn't it? What's real in America is everybody for himself.

Well, how can opportunity be equal unless you plunder from somebody else to begin with? Let's suppose now somebody says, "well, we want equality." Well, first of all now, in order for things to be equal, one group of people sends money into the treasury to benefit another group of people and that was sent in there by force; the only way equality can be gained is by force of one group against the other.

The issue is not merely cultural despair or political alienation, but the antipathy between the wider public interest and the narrow self-interest of big business.

You are right when you say the big corporations run the government and the country, and they run it in their interests. Nothing interferes with profits. Money is the American god. It's the corporations who ruined this beautiful country—polluted the rivers and the air. And they are still doing it. They don't give a damn for the health of the country. They do everything they can to sell us their products—including lying about how reliable they are. Have you noticed how everything you buy breaks sooner or later? That, they don't tell you about. And if the government does anything forcing them to clean up the environment or raises their taxes, nothing really happens. The laws never get passed. The rivers never get cleaned. Somewhere, somehow, big companies, big oil companies, and the telephone company escape. How do they find it? They must have control in Washington. They must finance campaigns or promise jobs or trips—I don't know how they do it, but they do it.

And the only thing we can hope for is to make them smaller—to break them up and force them to compete. Socialism is no good. The state always becomes a dictator and the people lose their freedom. So you can't do that.

All you can do is make the giant companies smaller and watch them and make them compete and punish them if they don't.

The symptoms of social decay are visible in the petty routines of daily life and the self-serving behavior of the state. Grammar school girls are pregnant. The law has become the shield of the guilty. There is fear of the night. Homes become fortresses to shut out life. Television replicates and exacerbates the most violent and sordid aspects of life. Parents have lost control of children. The school system cannot control pupils, many of whom drink and take drugs within earshot of their teachers. Big business, the model American profession, is responsive solely to its own interests, regardless of the nation's true need. The symptoms are obvious. But this catalog of despair and anger is far from complete. It is symptomatic, not definitive, of a more corrosive breakage.

Callers argue that they know the symptoms of the crisis but not the causes. Greed and selfishness, allegedly the efficient wellsprings of free enterprise, are commonly cited as causes. There is a strong sense that the traditional restraints on bourgeois hunger have become unbound. But talk radio, even in its most sophisticated moments, offers little explanation for the disappearance of selflessness. The common explanation for the cultural crisis is television, the domain of ego ideals that feature the sensuous, the rapacious, the very rich, and the lawman and the gangster. But this may be more predicate than subject. Callers widely believe that the old ways of doing things are dying and that the Protestant ethic is passé. Cheating in business has become common practice and corruption in government is the norm. The church is becoming peripheral, an archaic legacy that appeals primarily to the elderly and the repressed. Families are expendable. But no one know precisely how and why "selfishness is killing America." The symptoms are clear, but the diagnosis is vague.

There is, however, a consensus that greed has made people hostile and defensive. It has corrupted friendships, destroyed felicity, and created an uncaring America—a war of all against all.

But other malignancies exist, which feed upon each other and which have transformed a culture of equality and self-reliance into a pit of special interests. Social welfare, affirmative action, environmental protection, and moral relativism are the root causes of American ills. The problem for some is excessive self-interest, for others it is the publicly generated impediments to self-interest.

> Essentially, welfare causes poverty. It does this by subsidizing people to have more babies, by encouraging people not to work, by encouraging fathers to leave the home. Generally, welfare breaks up the family, breaks down the human character, and discourages human growth . . . welfare does not help people in poverty. It causes poverty and in turn causes crime.
>
> There are so many people like you say that are so busy and so exhausted from trying to meet their payments on houses and bills and everything, and putting kids through college, honest working people . . . I see a member of my family struggling and people around getting welfare, and keeping people that have to work all day up . . . these people don't work, they don't know what it's like to be civil. They have to put up with trash plus the government zinging them.

The conservative host and a black welfare recipient confront each other in a dialogue that exemplifies the conflict of two cultures and much of fury that lies behind Reaganism. The exchange also illustrates the capacity of political talk radio to capture the nuances of daily life.

> I was sleeping.
>
> You were sleeping. Come on, it's twenty-two minutes before nine. Up and at 'em.
>
> What?
>
> I said, It's twenty-two minutes before nine o'clock, up and at 'em.
>
> Don't you talk about putting people to work who's on welfare.
>
> Why not?
>
> What do you mean, why not? I'm not going to work.

Yeah, just have the paycheck sent home so you can sleep through the day, huh?

I'm waiting on the mailman now.

To get your paycheck?

Yeah. My check comes today.

Yeah. What's the matter with you? Why don't you work?

Because I don't want to work, that's why.

Oh, that's great. And what if the rest of the people don't want to work? Why should you be supported by people who work for a living?

I'm being paid reparations for my forefathers' work.

Your forefathers! Your forefathers didn't do anything for you. If they could see you now they'd spit on you.

They gave this country free labor for centuries.

You're—you—look at that as an excuse. You're a cop out!

I encourage all black people not to work.

Yeah, that's right, sure. You just sit back and say, you don't have to work because of what someone else did. You're good at that. You know, you know people who live off others—do you know what that's called? That's called being a parasite. You're a parasite.

I'm not going to work. As long as I get my welfare and my food stamps, that's all I care about.

You just sit back and you take it easy and other people who work for a living have to support you. I've got a question—what do you do with your time?

Just hang downtown, that's all. I walk around the Common, hang downtown, that's all.

Just take it easy. Gee, I'm sorry to get you up at this hour. It must be early for you. I don't know why you bother to get out of bed at all.

You get me upset when you mention you don't want people on welfare. Workfare was killed. I keep abreast of these matters when I hear people talk about cutting welfare.

That's probably the only time you show any energy in the day is when somebody's going to take away your check. If you showed that much enthusiasm for working you wouldn't have to be on welfare.

I don't want to work. I can't work for nobody else. It's time for me to collect reparations for centuries of slavery—

You didn't go through centuries of slavery, buddy.

—paid for that work.

We don't owe *you* anything. Because you're just a lazy punk. Listen to you now, you're just slurring your speech!

Got to go to this mailman waiting at the front door. I'll get up now. I'll see you later.

The host felt compelled to sermonize, to preach on the virtues of the self-reliance. His testament to labor was obviously shared by millions of mistrustful Democrats who opted for Social Darwinism and Reagan. After the caller hung up, the host continued his sermon.

All of you out there going to work, driving your cars, or if you're at home getting ready to get the kids off to school, you pay taxes—that's where your tax dollar is going. To support bums like that. And you heard him. He calls up and see—the only thing that got him riled was when I said let's put people like that back to work. And he has the nerve to say that he is owed something because of what happened to other people hundreds of years ago— black people. Well, there was discrimination and there were bad things that happened to some black people hundreds of years ago, although I know a lot of white people who had some rough going. But I'll tell you something—there's nobody on this planet who is responsible for that, and you cannot live off the backs of others, nor can you take claim for crimes that were committed against others and claim that therefore you deserve reparations, as he calls it. That's just a lot of hogwash. And what it does do is it justifies in his own mind why he can just lay back and just wait for the postman to come by with his check. It must be nice, huh? He must think of the rest of the people who work for a living as fools.

Welfare is the most provocative Democratic program, and the most useful to conservatives because it violates so many American norms and can be used to explain so many American failures: welfare causes poverty, encourages unemployment, unravels families, escalates crime, and stunts human developmet. Attributing these social ills to welfare frees the economy and the social system of responsibility. The commitment to free enterprise remains unquestioned. The purity of the system is reaffirmed by blaming the victim, not the system. The poor voluntarily opt for poverty and welfare, and are therefore responsible not only for their own misery, but for accelerating that misery and for the social problems that ensue.

Welfare is particularly galling because those who despise it must also pay for it. It is as if saints were forced to make transfer payments to sinners.

A bleeding heart is a person that seems to feel sorry for anybody that comes along and starts crying the blues. I would like to say that if you remember World War II, do you remember that we had people that wouldn't work even during the times that there were more jobs than we could possibly fill, we had the unemployable list, well we have the unemployable list today. But they want everything for nothing, and I'm very proud of our president and I'm a Democrat. I'm very proud of Mr. Reagan who will stand back and say, hey you people out there who aren't willing to work, then you're not willing to eat. You remember the old statement by St. Paul, he was one of our boys, "If you don't want to work, you don't eat" . . . I'm damn sick and tired of paying the bills for all these people who want to climb on the bandwagon for nothing.

> I think the party [the Republican Party] should divide
> [itself] into producers and nonproducers. I consider non-
> producers to be college professors, school teachers, and
> government employees in general, and people on the dole,
> what have you. Now they're the people who have a vested
> interest in having the government do something for them,
> and to hell with the cost to the people who have to pay
> for them, and the people who have to pay for it are the
> producers.

Pollsters report that very large numbers of people believe that the crisis of confidence was largely the result of too much selfishness— the failure of people to care for each other. Self-interest, the classic bourgeois virtue, is used to condemn the bourgeoisie. This extremely radical counterculture idea, the "un-American" core of the crisis, is also used to condemn the working-class unemployed. They, too, are greedy: "they want everything for nothing." The poor are condemned because they are rewarded, but perform no service.

There is a peculiar and comical reverse Marxism here. The world historical struggle is not between classes, but producers and nonproducers, the worthy and the unworthy, the parasite and the host. Capitalism, for Marx, was the triumph of exploitation by the rich. Capitalism, in the age of the welfare state, is the triumph of neither the capitalists nor proletarians, but the unemployed dregs of society. Deprived of the means of production, they prosper at the expense of all other classes.

> The Lord said unto the people, "This will be the manner
> of the King that shall reign over you. He will take his sons
> and appoint them unto him for his chariots and to be his
> horsemen and they shall run before his chariots. And he
> will appoint them unto him for thousands of thousands
> of years and to plow his ground and to reap his harvest
> and to make his instruments of war and the instruments
> of his chariots. And he will take his daughters to be per-
> fumers, and to be cooks and to be bakers . . . and he will
> take your menservants and your maidservants and your
> goodliest young men and put them to work." If you sub-
> stitute for the king, the government, and you have to

follow the biblical statements, the king will draft your sons, take your land, tax your behinds off and make you wives and daughters go to work—sure enough just like clockwork.

These burdens seem unconscionable to working men who realize that they must struggle for the benefit of parasites.

I was just listening to that punk that called in, and here I am breaking my neck to get into work, and guys like that can lie around in bed and collect a welfare check. . . . I have to work every day and have been working for years and have raised my children . . . it's terrible. The whole system needs changing because it's to easy to get a free handout, that's why people lie around in bed and brag. It just makes you sick.

Although blacks are perceived as the prime recipients of welfare and affirmative action, racism on talk radio is veiled. White callers have found more acceptable, artful, and American themes for condemning state aid than race hatred. Racism, for most callers, was not a significant issue until the federal judiciary insisted on integrated schools. This sweeping violation of public morals transformed whites into bigots.

Hatred was created by Judge Garrity [who ordered the integration of schools]. The Government can't solve anything. Even black people hate busing. I think it's demeaning to black people to be told that they must have affirmative action and busing. A lot of them don't like it. There shouldn't be special treatment. If government didn't interfere the economic opportunities would equal out. Blacks are as good as whites and can do it for themselves. Special programs teaches them they are inferior, special programs demeaning to blacks. Economic gains will solve black problems!!

These ideas are a rationale for capitalist revitalization, the core of neoconservatism. Government cannot solve complex economic problems because they result from disturbances of natural, immutable economic laws. Economic growth, unleashed by laissez faire, is the only solution, particularly because blacks are as competent as whites. They will prosper given the economic opportunity. Equality among the races is used here to reaffirm the virtues of captalism and diffuse the need for more affirmative action. State aid demeans blacks and destroys their self-reliance. The liberal cliché of the Democratic Party and its egalitarian ethic are counterproductive. They hinder the economic progress of blacks, who hate enforced equality, hate busing, and hate being treated as special. They, too, believe in hard work and self-reliance. The problem is to accelerate capital accumulation, not to provide contrived opportunity. This fusion of classic nineteenth-century liberalism and Social Darwinism is a very effective tool of social control, as well as a defense of capitalism. It refutes the case for special treatment of the dispossessed while reaffirming the virtues of laissez-faire. This approach obviates the need for openly racist argument. Many callers, however, believe that whites are now discriminated against. Affirmative action, designed to compensate for racism, actually recreates it in another form.

> I would like to talk about the government allowing us to be liberal and it takes away our responsibility. . . . The government I think is liberal and it takes responsibility onto others. It can strip us of our pride . . . for example the Constitution—I believe it's the Constitution, says that everyone's equal regardless of race, creed, and color, we know that's not true, it doesn't work that way. I am white and if I go for the job and there's a black person next to me and that company only has room for one person, I know damn well that the company will take that black person other than me, even if I have the qualifications. . . . I felt at the time that *Roots* [the television movie] was history, but I think the purpose of it going on the air was to make us feel very sorry for them, we will give them anything they want, consequently we strip them of their pride, they don't have to work or earn for what they get, they just get it because they're black.

The white argument centers around the virtues of the Protestant ethic and the violation of that ethic by blacks on welfare. On occasion, the agrument becomes openly racist. The host confronts a racist caller.

> You obviously don't like blacks, and I want to find out why.

> They don't work for one thing.

> They all don't work, right?

> That's right.

> And what else? Why don't they work?

> Why don't they work? Why the hell should they work when they're getting everything for nothing.

> Do you know that in this town two-thirds of the people on welfare are white?

> That's a phony argument, you're going on population. The conclusion I reach is that the government is giving them everything and they haven't given me that much.

> What does that indicate?

> It indicates poor leadership in this country.

> Racially inferior, they don't work, right.

> Right.

> And they just don't measure up to your standards.

> I don't know what my standard is, but it's a hell of a lot bigger than theirs, I've worked all my life for a living.

During the height of the discussion on social welfare, an instance of large-scale looting, allegedly by blacks, was reported in the press. This riot sharpened the debate and prompted the following remarks by the conservative host.

> It really is a zoo, it's really quite clear that there are some people in this society that have forfeited the right to live with civilized people, to live in a civilized society, a twen-

tieth-century society, they should be isolated and set apart from the rest of the community. Let them follow their jungle ways in some created jungle somewhere, that's fine, but get them away from the rest of us, decent people just deserve something better. That's how twisted and perverted the liberal mentality has become in these areas, that we're expected to put up with this [looting] in the name of civilization. This is not civilized.

A pattern of racism gradually emerged. The mistrust of America during the 1960s and 1970s was occasioned in large part, by the apparent reversal of traditional roles: blacks becoming more powerful and whites becoming less able to stop the process. The situation was particularly frustrating because the "transfer" of power was initiated by the Democratic Party, the party of the working class, and it had had the imprimatur of state power. It was as if the Democratic Party had reversed its traditional racist role at the expense of millions of its most staunch, though vulnerable, supporters.

One female caller, super-patriotic or psychotic, commented on the appointment of a black woman to the federal bench.

They appointed a black militant who defended Angela Davis . . . a black militant. What kind of justice is that? What the hell are we, communist here? They're trying to take us over. They hate the white people. . . . Martin Luther King . . . they're all communist . . . hired by the FBI but it was secretly hushed up, if you check back. And in this country we give him a holiday. Isn't that nice. Satan is going to walk the earth. He must enter into the body of a human being to work his will. I believe Satan entered into Martin Luther King's body. He was dead then.

The frustration that prompted much of the crisis is evident. Traditional values were eroding. The work ethic appeared to be under attack. Blacks, ethnics, and women demanded parity and the state opted to satisfy some of their demands, at much psychic and financial cost to the lower middle class, whose status was threatened by their safe passage from bondage. Anger mounted as inflation narrowed the already-marginal differences in income between competent and competitive working men and the indolent unemployed. Racism, a recessive strain, became virulent when rising unemployment made the American Dream appear to be a cruel deception.

The liberal host often became the displaced target of this lower-class frustration. A belligerent caller baits the host.

Why are you so against violence on TV and people with guns? Why don't you just come out of the closet? Everyone knows you're a closet homosexual.

Oh, how did you find out?

The way you were talking all that stuff against Anita [Bryant].

Now how did you find out? I was trying to hide it.

You're sure as hell not doin' it. Everybody knows what you are. . . . You're a fairy-lovin', nigger-lovin' Jew.

Anything else?

That pretty well covers it. Everyone knows what you are. I'm just tellin' 'em. Now your wife knows what you are.

What do you do for a living?

None of your business . . . unemployed. You know why? Because I'm white. And your industry, too . . . pretty soon it's gonna be taken over, too. You'll be down at the an-tique shop, dusting antiques, saying some jigaboo took my place. We'll see how you like it. Standin' in line for two hours to collect unemployment.

Ladies and gentlemen, you've heard the face of the hater. The bigot of the week. . . . Listen, do you live with yourself?

I live here with my family, by God, and I'll protect them to the end.

You have a family?

That's right, and I also have a gun.

Oh, really, that makes you a big man.

Listen, I'm tired of getting ripped off all the time. . . . I was in a civil service job and I was overqualified. . . . It's just too bad I was born white.

Your feeling sorry for yourself?

Heh, what you got to worry about man, you're a minority. You're a Jew. I'm sick of what's goin' on in this world.

You need a gun?

It gives me a little courage. I have more threats each day than you do in a lifetime. What do you expect, you love niggers? We were here first. You're forgettin' white people. You stick up for these minorities all the time.

You live in the city?

Yeah, in a house. I've lived here all my life.

What do you do for money? Are you on welfare?

I wouldn't go on welfare if they paid me.

What do you do, steal?

My wife had to go out and get a job.

Why don't you go out and get a job? That's what you tell people on welfare.

It's a pretty darn disgrace in this country. . . . You go to the bank and count all your money, 'cause I know about all you Jews.

There is a liberal and a conservative diagnosis of the crisis of confidence. The liberals mistrust unbounded self-interest—greed if you will—and believe that it has created a society in which the common good has been inundated by narrow, private calculations of material success. The particular has triumphed over the universal. In this hierarchy of values, the cause of public service and mutual aid has become peripheral. Hostile and social relations and antisocial activities have become peripheral. the norm, imposed on the society by unmitigated self-interest. The liberals are wary of the bourgeois aspects of human nature that Marx described; they have not, however, relinquished their commitment to free enterprise or competition. They are wary, but not despairing.

Conservative callers mistrust America because the republic is abandoning its traditional reliance on the virtues that self-interest unleashes. Government regulation of the economy and society has created a nation beset by forced and artificial privilege, fused with inequality and inequity, a society in which the virtues of self-reliance and individualism are being replaced by dependence and indolence. The individual is losing his pride because the state guarantees a living regardless of competence. The Darwinian struggle for existence, the most solid basis of progress, has been violated. Initiative, persistence, and hard work no longer bring their just reward. The Protestant ethic, backbone of the republic, has been destroyed by an abstract and impractical liberal philosophy that elevates the category, the group, the race, over the individual.

The conservative's retinue of evils is large: environmental tampering, public fraud, the destruction of self-reliance, sexual permissiveness, immorality, unequal opportunity, and the decline of public education—all primarily caused by state interference or incompetence. Conservative callers are not immune from fear of conspiracy. Their arguments have, at times, a paranoid style. Powerful, insidious, and amoral forces are at work: environmentalists who are actually communists, disarmament advocates who aid the Soviet Union, public policy experts who venerate collectivity at the expense of individuals. Their argument is strident and couched in moralistic and uncompromising dualities. Politics for many conservative callers has become religion, as exemplified by the callers quoted below.

You've got to talk a bit about the mentality of what's going on, these people [environmentalists] are anti- the capitalist system, they're anti-free enterprise, they are left-wing in terms of their politics—it is exactly the same kind today.

You're quite right, it's the newest issue that they're trying to drum up support for. The reason that they're against nuclear technology is not because they give a hoot or

holler over the ocean . . . polution is not their concern. What they want to do is see that the United States doesn't develop any more energy sources so that the United States becomes a weaker country, that's the real objective.

You see them [environmentalist] walking down here with their little letters to the governor against Edison, and they're out and out socialists, at least they're hiding behind the cloak of socialism, we all know what's behind the cloak, but anyway, one stopped me and he said, "Oh you believe in Rockefeller being on welfare!" And I said, "Now look, you go from the sublime to the ridiculous." I said Rockefeller isn't on welfare. I said I don't dislike people because they happen to be wealthy, because a man might have 10, 20, or 50 million dollars. All my life I've worked, I didn't go out and get a fancy education like they [environmentalists] did, because I had to go out and support my mother after my father died. I deeply resent these people and I just hope to God they're listening. The blue-collar worker, the guy that's working for a living is not behind you, and he's not behind your communistic, socialistic, stupid ways, and if they ever try it, if they ever try to take this country any other way . . . they're going to lose.

These kids [Seabrook protestors] by and large never had to work for anything, that's why they don't have much and that's why they don't have the respect for anybody else who has worked hard for everything.

Let me tell you something, I'm getting a little tired of these creeps. . . . I'm far from being a blue-collar worker, but I work, I don't know where these guys come from, I don't know what they're thinking, Avi [Nelson, the host], but the average guy, he's probably out working two jobs to pay his electric bills, while these guys are out there sitting in someone's field [Seabrook Nuclear Power Plant] sitting on someone's private property. . . . Well, it's about time we start making them have respect. I'm telling you,

if they come and sit on my property, they're going to get
a thirty-three bullet in the head.

Private property and self-reliance, the twin virtues of the capitalist
tradition, evoke from conservatives super-patriotic defense when the
state seeks, even in modest ways, to limit those virtues through
restraints on business. Conservatives are acutely interested in any
misuse of government funds designated for the underclass, because
fraud proves that state interference creates more problems than it
solves. Fraud also reaffirms the parisitism and criminality of the
underclass. Stories of fraud and self-indulgence among the supposedly indigent abound on political talk radio when a guest or the host
cites some outrageous abuse of welfare or affirmative action. The
circle of stories and gossip widens and becomes more credible as
callers report their personal knowledge of wrong doing.

There are many things wrong with governmental programs designed to help the poor, not the least of which
is fraud.
  I would advise him and others in government looking
for fraud to investigate subsidized housing. There is another Pandora's box If you know anything about subsidized housing, which Reagan has cut back on
tremendously. But it's still alive and well here in the Commonwealth. We have young people down on the water-
front working in the offices living in luxury apartments,
being subsidized by you and me, and the elderly housing,
you wouldn't believe the cars that drive up there to visit.
  I'll tell you a scenario that's repeated quite often in this
elderly housing. Mom and Dad will sell the house, and
they'll give it to Junior or the daughter, and they'll say:
Mom or Dad, you go into elderly housing, and the tax-
payers will subsidize your rent, your heat, your utilities,
and you'll get food stamps also, you give us the money,
we'll get a nice house, a new car, etc.

More solid proof of fraud was provided by a bank teller who reports
that many depositors cash their welfare checks and paychecks
simultaneously.

I work for a bank down in the ghetto. And I wish I had a dollar for everybody that cashed their welfare check with their paycheck and oooh.

I'll tell you something, you know what you ought to do?

I thought of it. I can't involve the bank. I wanted to report all of them and I started a list—I got twelve names of paychecks with welfare checks and I said, "Well I'll be damned, I'm going to turn these people in. Right!" Names, social security numbers, and everythng. I turned a couple of them in.

Yeah, but you don't have to involve the bank. All you have to do it just say, here you are an anonymous good guy doing a service for the Commonwealth.

They still keep cashing those checks, though. Every one of them. Not one of them has stopped.

How long ago did you turn them in?

Already three or four months ago. Now I'm at the point where I don't even bother.

Yeah, well, I care about it. I want you to do me a favor, all right?

Sure.

I don't like when I hear stuff like that. I am sick and tired of hearing how people are ripping off the taxpayer to collect welfare illegally. I want you to give me the names of those people, all right, I'm going to trust that you— you're going to be honest with me, right?

I'll give you the names.

All right. And I'll take them to welfare and I want to see what they do about it. How's that. And then we'll follow it on the air. We'll have a conversation periodically with the welfare people to see how well they're doing picking up on the fraud that's costing the taxpayer money. Don't identify the bank is it? Which bank do I go to and cash

my checks? You know what they'll start doing—cashing
their checks at separate banks.

This is the militant host, the moralistic and self-righteous judge,
always hoping to purify the wellspring of public morality by casting
out the sinners. His desire to punish and his sense of justice appeal
enormously to the conservative audience. The personal experience
of the bank teller is incontrovertable proof of the conservative scenario. This stark moralistic posture resonates with the audience. The
host provides another instance in which government incompetence
subverts social justice.

The Labor Department and the Department of Commerce
were persuaded to give $700,000 of tax money to teach
minority youth how to silk-screen t-shirts, a complicated
two-hour course. The promoters call this Giant Step In-
corporated. Giant Step produced apparently 100 percent
nothing results. Senator William Proxmire, who keeps track
of these things, you know he has the Golden Fleece Award,
etc., pointed out that not one t-shirt was produced for
sale, not one minority youth found a job, only seventy-six
trainees enrolled, none received usable training, and of
the thirteen that were said to have graduated, half did
not know they had finished the program . . . bright guys,
no doubt, H.L. Mencken, who was a great American jour-
nalist and satirist, pointed out a very fundamental political
truism—what men value in this world are not rights, but
privileges. The Democrats have learned that and imple-
mented it for years, it is the way you buy political elections,
you offer people privileges, you don't talk about defend-
ing their rights, because most people don't want just rights,
they want largesse, and if it means at someone else's expense, well that's just peachy keen, too.

Affirmative action, an evil child spawned by Democratic intellec-
tuals, confirms, for many callers, Mencken's theory of democracy.
One caller presented the case against affirmative action.

The fire department was the case in point . . . ad on the
front page of the *Lynn Item*, two ads that appear side by

side, one in English and one in Spanish. Become a fire-fighter—it goes on to say job security, fringe benefits, retirement program, advancement opportunities, ample vacancies, starting salary $12,956. Then it goes on to say that the City of Lynn is conducting a special minority recruiting program. Exam may be taken either in English or Spanish. At the very bottom of it it says, "An equal opportunity employer."

First of all, as a taxpayer I resent the fact that these government agencies always have to put their ads on the front page of the paper, when private enterprise can't afford it, they have to go on the inside of the paper. But I called the publisher of the *Lynn Item* the other day when I was so irked by this, and I said where does the general public have to go for recourse on fraudulent, deliberate fraudulent advertisement, in your paper. Of course he asked me what it was about, and I told him it was contradictory. It said that the exam may be in English and Spanish, number one, and it says "equal opportunity employer." How about Armenian, Hungarian, in Bulgarian and all the others, and number two, they're singling out minorities. So, being the radical that I am, I called the chief of the fire department, and of course he had to take a neutral position. But I said, what would happen if this test can be given in Spanish, what would happen that a woman whose house is on fire yells out the window, "My children are in the back bedroom"? He'd just scream back, "No speaka English." Yes, he doesn't understand. Then what would happen in a case like that? You see. And I think what's happening is that the middle, hard-working American in this country, the middle class, is becoming the minority.

The cry is social injustice. The American Dream has been shattered. The state has dismantled the Protestant ethic; the poor prosper at the expense of the rich. The indolent feast at the table of labor. The crisis of confidence was, in large part, a negative response to the American dream of equality, a dream that became a nightmare when it became clear that equality for some necessitated economic sacrifice for others.

But the mistrust of America did not stem solely from economic uncertainty or injustice. Moral relativism and permissiveness in the schools were destroying learning and the virtue of individualism. The judiciary promoted crime by perversely extending the rights of the accused. Liberal regulation of the economy and environmentalism sapped the strength of free enterprise. Social welfare cheapened the individual, sapped his pride, destroyed his self-reliance, created poverty by promoting indolence, shattered the family, and accelerated sexual license and crime. This neoconservative chamber of horrors, the agenda of Reaganism, occasions a simple political philosophy: the state cannot solve problems; only economic growth can relieve social distress. State regulation breeds more state regulation. Bureaucracy expands exponentially. The state and individual freedom are natural enemies. State interference hampers self-interest and free enterprise, so that they cannot unleash prosperity and a variety of social harmonies. The state promotes the plunder of one class by another. The viability of the American Dream is the issue.

Well, how can opportunity be equal unless you plunder from somebody else to begin with? Let's suppose now somebody says well, we want equality. Well, first of all now, in order for things to be equal, one group of people send money into the treasury to benefit another group of people and that was sent in there by force, the only way equality can be gained is by force on one group against the other.

[The host reaffirms the theory of reverse Marxism.]

Pretty soon we'll have half the population working for the other half. Then, they can vote itself raises from the other half's production. Leave the rest of us alone. If we want to take saccharine, we should be able to. If we want to we should be able to choose to smoke cigarettes, drink alcohol, or smoke marijuana. The eventual conclusion is the government takes over, like the Soviet Union.

Mistrust of America is contagious; the confidence gap spreads from politics to big business, to the press, to the professions, and to the schools. According to many callers there is a domino effect, in which bits and pieces of state control lead to total control.

> I don't know if they are socialists or communists or just plain stupid. All this government intervention. All these programs. You can't move without a government regulation. You can't take pills unless they say it's okay. You can't drink after a certain hour. You can't send your kid to the school you want to. You can't employ who you want to or fire who you want to. You can't sell something—below a certain price. A permit to do this. A permit to do that. But you can get an abortion, or get a job if you're black or Puerto Rican regardless of whether you got the stuff. Or you can get welfare and not do anything. And who do you think pays for all of this? What the hell happened to this country? What about free enterprise, a day's pay for a day's work? We're becoming a dictatorship to help bums and parasites, and the judges just go along.

> We've got a bunch of spender-nuts down there. I think they're just too stupid to try to socialize us. I think they're socializing us unconsciously. I think they're a bunch of nuts. . . . They're either stupid or downright devils. You can take your choice. If it's a conscious conspiracy then it makes me even more angry. What I wanna know is when the American electorate is gonna wake up and kick these bums.

The issue is not merely dictation and force; it is powerlessness, the inability to control one's life, the inability to counter immoral and financially debilitating forces. The conservative host alerts his audience.

> The problem has to do with basic morality and basic philosophy. The problem is small children are being forced on a school bus against their wishes and against the wishes

of their parents. He may not want his kid on the bus because the bus is painted yellow. That should be his right.

Callers are quick to calculate the infringements on individual freedom that, when taken in sum, amount to dictatorship.

Now, I don't like dictation from the government. Federal money is being used for this so we are all affected. This is dictation. We have to nip it in the bud. I think one of the most important things about this antibusing movement . . . they aren't allowing politicians to have any leadership in the organization.

The crisis of confidence is ultimately a crisis of powerlessness, precipitated by the belief that the individual has become a pawn of external forces that are beyond his control and not always identifiable. When feelings of powerlessness are fused with a profound sense of social injustice, the burden becomes heavy and the mistrust becomes pervasive. Despair is compounded by the suspicion that there may be no easy remedy. The conservative callers, however, believe that the restoration of free enterprise and unrestrained self-interest might resolve the American crisis

The conservative host addressed the issue when a caller asked, "Would you define what libertarian is and explain why it is more consistent than other philosophies."

Okay, all right, I'll do that. A libertarian is someone who believed in the principle of individual freedom and holds it on both the civil issues or social issues and the economic issues. . . . as far as definitions go the libertarian—although there is a wide variation in lifestyles—generally subscribes to the credo that it is immoral to initiate the use of force against another human being to obtain a value. And that means a libertarian subscribes to the belief that, for example, if you have a company you should be able to hire whom you please, that if you have a home, you should be able to sell it to whom you please, that you and I, if we choose to enter into some kind of voluntary negotiated agreement, that nobody should put that asun-

der, that the government should not step in and say,
"You've violated what we consider to be a legitimate contract, therefore we're throwing it out." You shouldn't be
forced to have seat belts in your car. And you shouldn't
be forced to have a certain percentage of people of a
particular skin configuration in your employment.

Now, all of these things so far I've talked about are
things that a conservative would agree with, but a liberal
probably would not. Now let's go to the other side: the
use of marijuana. A libertarian would say, "If somebody
wants to use marijuana, that's his business." The liberal
would agree. The conservative would not. When it comes
to pornography, the libertarian would say, "Look, if he
wants to read it, and he engaged in a voluntary trans-
action with somebody who sold the book, that's okay."
The liberal would agree; the conservative would not. So
what do you have? You have the libertarian agreeing with
the liberal on social issues and agreeing with the conservative on economic issues.

What it comes down to is that the libertarian maintains
a consistent perspective on individual liberty, maintaining
that somebody who does things voluntarily with another
person should be able to do that and the government
should not intrude. And that's what makes it more consistent a philosophy; it's more consistent philosophically.
It doesn't necesarily, in and of itself, make it better socially—in the sense that it's going to necessarily lead to
a better society. Personally, I think it will. But the conservatives and the liberals would also say, "yes, we believe
in freedom up to a point, because we think there are
certain needs that society has and therefore we must restrict people's behavior in certain conditions." And you've
probably been hearing, if you've been listening to the
program recently, people calling up and wanting to restrict people's freedom in the area of pornography, and
you hear liberals call up and want to restrict people's freedom in economic areas. But that makes them inconsistent
philosophically.

Forty years of the New Deal, the Fair Deal, and the Great Society, of social and economic reform, evoke a reaction: a historical cycle in which the nation seems to demand a respite from social change, a time to consolidate and permit the natural sequences of time, place, and self-interest to reaffirm themselves. One cycle appears to exhaust and disabuse itself through excess government control or incompetence, while another affirms the need for retrenchment and a reversal of contemporary history. The new era heralded by callers to talk radio is introduced in moralistic and strident terms: the demand is for total reconstruction of the social order. The extremism of the past necessitates the extremism of the present. Political talk radio of the late 1970s and early 1980s is not merely an oral history of the crisis of confidence, but a signal of the end of one cycle and the beginning of another. Conservative talk radio, and—more significantly—much liberal talk, is a catalog of the despair, hope, and remedy that became Reaganism—the contemporary cycle of reaction.

Much of the force of this reaction arose from the belief that liberals had destroyed the American Dream.

The thing that I am so resentful of is that we built this house ourselves, we intended to live in it in our old age, and we are being forced to leave it. If we had decided to leave it of our own free will, that would be one thing. But we can't afford to live here once my husband is retired. The inequities are the thing. . . . If everybody else had been assessed fairly I think we would not all have been hurt as badly as we have. The inequities have been horrendous. I don't know what the answer is. The answer for us is flight. We've just got to get out as fast as we can. They [the assessors] double-talk you right out of the office. If the formula is fair and square, an intelligent person should be able to sit down and assess their own house. But if I can't do it then there's something wrong. And I never have been able to get a straight answer to this question. We should all be able to know how they have arrived at the figures they have given us. And they can't do this. My blood boils when I think about this because I resent the fact that they're pushing me out, they're push-

ing me out of Massachusetts. There's nothing I can do
about it . . . this is the destruction of a dream.

The dream was built on hard work and thrift, and on the assumption that the state would fulfill its fiduciary obligation. The
dream could be realized while the economy expanded, and people
could believe they influenced state policy through elections that offered meaningful choices. When economic conditions became more
constrained, people perceived the change as a political failure. The
crisis of confidence was in large part a political crisis, an overwhelming belief in the unresponsiveness of American political institutions.
The state, for many, was the prime cause of American's difficulties.
Politics was no longer considered a viable medium for social change.

> Change in this country doesn't come about quick enough.
> If the majority of the people both in the state and the
> country had the final say in all matters of legislation. . . .
> Aren't we powerful enough in this country? Don't we live
> in democracy? But people don't have the final say. I don't
> know! But my answer is that average working people
> should be in position of power. I don't think the politicians
> or the people in power have any relationship with me or
> you or the average guy in the street.

> I'd like to start a movement and call it TRO. Throw the
> rascals out. . . . Every incumbent is a rascal. Politicians
> are treating the citizens with contempt. . . . All of them
> from the local alderman all the way up to the president.

American politics reflects American society. It is a cockpit of self-
interest and manipulation, a game in which insiders prosper with
little regard for law and morality, yet, rarely pay the price.

> All these people that keep calling in on [Bert] Lance. They
> can't do a damn thing about it. He should resign. . . . I
> do believe that we can go out and vote and vote, but
> who do you know, everybody does it, everybody does it!
> From the lowest guy on up, and you know who gets
> caught? The little guy all the time. I see it in the govern-

ment, they don't let them get away with anything, and
the big guys can walk away with the building. . . . it will
be forever.

The rhetoric of mistrust is absolute: everyone in power violates
moral prescriptions and the law. "Big guys" never get caught. All
blacks are stripped of their pride. Welfare helps no one. Poverty is
always caused by welfare. One caller remarked, "Everything is for
criminals." Another lamented, "Everything good we no longer have."
Parents have lost all control of schools. America is not merely in
trouble, it is, as one caller said, "going to be buried." Another,
commenting on the national mood, remarked, "Everybody wants
everything." "The government can't solve anything." Subsidized
housing is a "Pandora's box" of corruption.

There are no shades of meaning, no qualifications or exceptions,
no tentativeness. The struggle to redeem America is total because
the enemies of America are energetically trying to reconstruct every
corner of American life. There is more than a bit of fear of conspiracy
here, more than a tinge of paranoia, nourished by the host's hyper-
bolic scenarios of Doomsday. The bellicosity of neoconservatism
stems from the belief that the liberal state has violated the foundations
of social justice. The apocalyptic character of neoconservative rhetoric stems from the belief that the Democratic Party effectuated a
transformation of social policy so profound and destructive that it is
almost irremediable.

The sense that the state is no longer interested in social justice
can energize the demand for social change. But the most effective
demands for change are rooted in the victimizations of daily life.
People become politically conscious when their children's education
is threatened or when they are displaced on the job for reasons they
believe to be discriminatory. Political consciousness is aroused when
people believe they are taxed for malicious or counterproductive
purposes, or when the meaningfulness of their family, work, or
religion is threatened by drastic social or political change. The erosion
of legitimacy occurs primarily within these contours. The state is
held in contempt primarily when it threatens or degrades the most
common experiences.

The crisis of confidence of the 1960s and 1970s was, in large part,
a response to such disturbances. The efforts to desegregate public

schools, alter the curriculum, and reduce parental control were perhaps the most threatening of these incursions. Here confidence in
the state turned to hatred; here racial and cultural conflicts exploded.
The mistrust of white Americans was fed by the assault on self-
reliance, the evils of moral relativism and permissiveness, and the
demise of learning.

Two pedagogues report on the culture of the schools, the seedbed
of the future.

A big mistake is we accepted a lowering of our standards
in society, for quite a few years now, keeps going down,
down, down. We don't have as much influence on our
children as their peers. I don't have much authority, but
what I do is I keep pointing out the mistakes that people
make. Now, I came in this afternoon and I had seen three
cars deliberately going through red lights. There were
young children crossing, elderly people on their crutches,
and it seems that they just have no regards for rights.
And, unless you bring a policeman to stand there, then
you're just taking your life in your hands.

I just smack them down, and they don't do it a second
time. If they do it a second time. . . . Still do it. But, you
know, I get beautiful results. I get no back talk. I don't
get anything. In fact, I've even got thanks from some of
the parents, because it tamed them down, too. The school
system's the way it is. They have no control over the kids.
The kids act like animals out of their trees. Don't let them
get away with vulgar language, dirty gestures, and all that
junk. People who get work all the time, they don't report
the kids. They get along fine. The headmasters, department heads, assistant headmasters, they don't want to be
bothered with that stuff, so long as the kids aren't both-
ering the class next door or somebody fighting or destroying public property.

All that Dr. Spock stuff is bull. It's too much permissiveness
that's causing the problem and the brutality and violence
of television. There is absolutely no discipline in the schools

at all. The administration doesn't want to hear about it. It takes up too much time.

You kid with the kids and use reverse psychology on them. You cannot touch them, you cannot. . . . The only thing that can happen to them is they can get suspended for five days, bring the parents up, and they're right back out doing the same thing. They drink in the school, smoke right in the school, snort cocaine in the schools . . . they go on. The honest God's truth. Our kids seem to have good tastes—they bring in Smirnoff Vodka, VSO. They bring in Chivas Regal, and there's drug dealing going on all over the place. My simple philosophy is why make waves? If I try something, I'll wind up just like the slob who was fired.

A concerned parent laments the loss of parental control. The conservative host then raises the issue of social control.

But parents are no longer responsible about what happens on their premises. . . . We didn't have any problems with drugs when I was young.

We are cheapening the individual. We tell him what he should eat, what he shouldn't eat. Whether he should wear seat belts or not. Lots of talk about the individual, but what has happened, in reality, the individual has been cheapened by society. There is no education going on in the school now. They don't teach the kids to achieve. They teach them to be socialized, to fit in. They teach them that if you are an inventor, your idea belongs to everybody, it just doesn't belong to you. If we don't prize the individual, if we don't value the individual, then the kid is not going to value the individual, and he is going to treat his own life cheaply. It's the fault of the system. It's a pervasive thing. Certainly the educational system would deserve a fair amount of blame. The parents as well.

The callers are quite sure that parental discipline accounted for much of their success, but they do not understand why the situation changed.

What happened to respect? When I was a kid, I respected
my parents and my parochial school teachers. They said,
we obeyed. They were authorities to us. I've been wondering why we had such respect and I think the answer
is that they limited us, set rules of behavior, standards,
and they enforced them with some punishment. We knew
what we could get away with and what we couldn't do.
And there was no question. I think this discipline was good
for me. I came to know who I was and who they were
and it was clear-cut. And I had a very good idea of what
was right and wrong. I don't know what happened, but
it's not like that now.

The host, more schooled in the complexities of social theory than
most of the callers, explains what happened.

Parents who try to hold the line find themselves to be an
island in a sea of permissiveness so that it becomes almost
impossible, to decide that their kids will live by a completely separate set of values. . . . Kids now are almost
a living suicide. . . . Parents don't have enough control.

It's the educators, not the parents, who have gone off the
deep end with this stuff, this new experimental education,
new math, new this, this nonsense about secular humanism. Our people don't have to learn, they have to fit in,
That's hogwash . . . this moral relativism . . . this secular
humanism nonsense . . . which is part of a modern educational theory, that the professional educators have
gravitated to. It is extremely left-wing and it talks about
making the child fit into society. Everything becomes relative . . . for example, . . . children are asked if it is always wrong to steal. And the answer is no. Should you
steal? Well, that depends on the situation. There is a moral
relativism. Morality is relative. There is no objective standard nor morality. . . . This is nonsense. You shouldn't
steal because that's just wrong. You talk about basic human rights and one of them is property rights. . . . The
object of the school is not to read and write but fit in, to

be socialized. It amounts to political propaganda, not education. In a few years, people won't recognize their kids.

Parents sense that permissiveness and moral relativism are related to lower academic standards, but are puzzled by the fact that traditional instruction has not been revived.

For two years now I have been reading that children who have gone off to school studying the new math are two years behind the children who normally studied the old math. I can't understand why the subject never comes up with parents and why the school systems haven't done something to go back to the old math.

The host again explains.

Well, it does come up on occasion, and people are getting a little fed up with the whole situation. You're right, we should go back to the old math—as a matter of fact, I think we should go back to the days where parents had a greater say in the child's education in terms of the curriculum, in terms of the atmosphere of the school, including discipline codes, dress codes, etc. The problem is, of course, that our kids have been used as guinea pigs, and every time some sociologist or some educational professional comes up with a new idea, he goes down to Washington, he persuades some office to give him a grant, and before you know it you find this garbage creeping into the schools. And what has happened as a result of that? You've got people who can't write an English sentence graduating from high school, you've got people who can't add, well, a little bit, too hot and heavy on that. But they don't know much about basic arithmetic or mathematics when they graduate, and it's really a sad commentary and I don't see why it is that we continue to allow the educational professionals to hold dominance over our kids.

The cheapening of the individual is not exclusively the work of schools. The government also compromises the work ethic and degrades personal achievement through affirmative action.

I see people whose labor productivity has gone down increasingly over this great period of welfare economics over the last twenty or thirty years. We're just not a productive country any more. We're just not as productive as we used to be, everyone can sense it, you just don't get the full day's work for the full day's pay.

Of course there are other things that are happening— let's be honest about this, unions I don't think have contributed a hell of a lot to productivity recently. We have special programs like affirmative action, the best guy is not selected for the job, and that produces more than just a bad selection, that produces an ethos in this country, that somehow excellence isn't the criterion to be strived for. We have programs where women are supposed to get special treatment . . . standards are being abridged so that we can get certain classes of people on. There's nothing productive about that, the work ethic has been compromised, and it shows, it's showing up in any number of places. The inefficiency isn't only in the work force. EEOC, programs like that, where you're going to make decisions on the basis of other than qualifications, on the basis of skin color, or genitalia, you're not going to end up with the most productive worker.

The tenor of these calls is clear. America has undergone an inversion, a pernicious transfer of values, in which evil has replaced good, parasitism has replaced productivity, and discrimination for the few has replaced equity for the many. The corrosion spreads from one aspect of public life to another, and this escalation generates and regenerates mistrust, leading the mistrustful to discover ever more social disorder. Criminality and sexual permissiveness preoccupy liberal and conservative callers. They are the ultimate consequences of liberal indulgence.

An angry caller, typical of many, develops the neoconservative theory of crime.

It makes me sick. That's why we've got so much crime in this country. Criminals have so many rights, that it's easy for a policeman to overlook some rights, and then a liberal judge lets these crooks off so they can return to the streets and rob somebody else. The Democrats keep appointing these liberal judges and the crime rate keeps rising. I am not opposed to a fair trial, but let's not bend over backwards. Enough's enough.

The mistrustful, prone to envision all social problems as catastrophic, contrast their powerlessness with the enormity of evil. "Everything is for the criminals these days, and there's not much you can do about it."

Homosexuality and gay rights evoke more bitterness and a more punitive stance than any other issue. Homosexual teachers pose the most immediate threat.

I don't want homosexuals teaching in schools. A boy might have a homosexual teacher and think this is the right way to go, or it might make someone who is not a homosexual think about it. If I were teaching, particularly in a boys' school, you would always have to worry that they found out about it and go home and tell their parents that you bothered them. The boys don't have protection for themselves. Homosexuals will favor the boys over the girls.

Shouldn't you be able, for example, to make a decision about hiring somebody on the basis of that person's homosexuality? And of course, the next step in this was there was already a discussion, already legislation passing in Massachusetts—about that homosexuals should be able to adopt children—a homosexual couple. Now I maintain that, for example, in the school, if I'm a parent and I want my child to receive an education, that part of the education is not only the textbook, but comes from the teacher and his style. And I would not want to see my guy come in smoking a pipe and wearing a dress and teaching my youngster—whatever it is he's teaching because I think that something is going to rub off from that particular attitude. And although I would grant him and defend his

right to act that way, I think I should be able to stay apart
from him.

On occasion, the host will devote an entire show to homosexuality
an invite a homosexual minister or psychologist as a guest. The topic
frequently stirs callers with strong religious convictions. "The Bible
says: if there is a man who lies with a male as those who lie with a
woman, both of them committed a detestable act, and they shall
surely be put to death."

The liberal host interjects, "Who said that? . . . People always
quote the Bible, but they never quote who said it."

"Oh, I'm not sure . . . Romans 25. If they exchange the truth of
God for a lie, and worship and serve the creature other than the
Creator."

Biblical exigesis is not a common occurrence on political talk radio,
but the guest is a lesbian minister.

Those verses are very important. If you will look at them
very carefully, and understand them. Now, realize that if
you're going to quote me Romans I, you also have to read
Romans II, because they're connected. And it says in the
first verse of Romans II, "and so will many of you, and
what right have you to judge the brother or sister, because
you're doing the same thing." Now you may not be gay,
but you're committing many, many sins, and what they're
talking about is sin in general. Not just sexual sins, but all
kinds of sins. And people have to realize that judging each
other is as great a sin as homosexuality. There's no such
thing as unforgivable sin, except the sin against the Holy
Spirit. So, you can't say that this sin is any worse than any
other sin. And the sin of pride, and the sin of hatred, and
the sin of condemnation of people is just as great a sin
as any kind of sexual sin. And Jesus Christ never said "I'm
only going to die for people who have never sinned."

This exchange beautifully illustrates the opportunity that talk radio affords both callers and listeners to develop a political identity,
to locate several aspects of an argument, to align themselves for or
against the topic under discussion. Talk radio provides a context that

permits a listener to know if he stands alone or has support. Talk radio exposes listeners to narrow and to tolerant dialectic—dialectic perhaps not developed elsewhere. This argument and counterargument replicates the agora, the Greek public square where debate on the public good defined the state and where civility was enlarged through participation in that debate. The enlargement of political civility in America is impossible because the urge to socialize—that is, liberalize—has displaced the need to debate.

A good example of the capacity of talk radio to enlarge the vision of listeners was provided by the minister who defended homosexuality.

> Our attitude toward gay people is occasioned by how we feel about death. We realize that gay people are probably not going to continue the race. And for many people it is very frightening to realize that if there were more gay people, the race would die out. And a *lot of us are terribly afraid* of death and anything that has to do with death. And so we are desperately afraid of gay people, who are not reproducing. And that says something to us about our own sense of dying out and not leaving anything behind. And if we would realize that so much of society's view of the gay person is conditioned by the old Hebraic fear of the race dying out, then we would be more tolerant of people than we are.

The fear and loathing of homosexuality and alternative lifestyles evoke more venom on talk radio than the welfare state or any other issue. The threat to America posed by deviance is apparently beyond calculation. The liberal host is bombarded by his more rigid callers when the subject arises.

> On the air, you promote, corrupt, this is going to corrupt the minds and bodies of the young. And it's wrong, and what you're telling the people out there, Jerry [Williams, the host], and this guy you have on, is that, what you're saying is, enter in the habits of perversion. And let me tell you it's small minds of men like you to promote this type of perversion. I think you're a disgrace. I wish that they'd

take you off the air because what you're doing . . . you're promoting gay rights, which isn't moral, it's perversion! It isn't right, it never will be right, so why don't you just get off it, and leave it be and stop promoting it. You know, Jerry, what you want? I'll tell you what you want. You want bands of homosexuals marching the streets, perverting the young. . . . Now listen here. They should take you off the air—you're a disgrace, promoting that kind of stuff. And furthermore, it won't go anywhere.

The conservative host entertains a guest who discusses alternative lifestyles. The callers are not cordial.

You're nuts. You're a disgrace to the United States. . . . You shouldn't have him on the program. It brings the United States into the mud. I don't want to talk any more, cause I'll have to talk to him some more. It's all I've got to say.

And what about the family? Isn't that the basic unit, children being educated correctly by parents, being loved by parents. This extramarital sex, or whatever you have—four people—it will destroy people's love. Most people cannot take that. They get angry and jealous, and the kids get badly treated. And there is bitterness and jealousy. God created marriage for a very good reason, and staying together. Your views will destroy all that. You're a dangerous man.

So would you say to a Jesuit father that alternative sexual lifestyles are moral! I think he would pound your head in . . . pound his head in. What you said, Avi. . . . Khrushchev was right. We're gonna be buried by these guys.

A minority of callers are tolerant toward homosexuality. Talk radio is rarely monolithic.

Take the relation between those who are vehement about the abortion issue and this issue. I think the people who are full of hate are really full of hang-ups, sexual hang-ups. And somehow they've been brought up by a code that they hate it, but they follow that code, and now they simply cannot readdress themselves to any other way of thinking . . . It's a manifestation of people being unhappy with their own lives. And I think they strike out when they're not happy with their own lives. I don't think it's the swingers that are . . . I think you're talking to people who are just generally unhappy and have to vent their anger in some way. So it focuses on people who have had abortions. Maybe some woman who had a baby and she suffered with this kind of thing, and so she strikes out. And maybe it's the same thing here. Maybe these people have latent homosexual feelings. I don't know. I mean, maybe I'm going too far in that direction, but I think that's what we have to do as a nation is own up to our own.

Callers to the conservative talk show are more strident than their liberal counterparts. Their disgust with the sexual revolution, one of the events that precipitated the crisis of confidence, is clear in this interchange initiated by the conservative host.

Take homosexual, that's what it means. I remember when it became slang and sort of abbreviated and they used to call them "homo"—just like that, and that would take care of it.

What was that?

Just the first part of the word, h-o-m-o, that was the slang that was used when I was younger.

Well, then we always used the word "queer".

Yes, queer; of course, "queer" takes a word from the language, too. Someone called yesterday and made, I thought a very interesting point. He said the whole discussion—the tone of the discussion—changes if instead of discussing "gay rights" you start discussing "queer rights."

Exactly, I'm glad someone else said that; I didn't catch the show . . .

The crisis of confidence is based, in part, on the perception that an illegitimate transfer of power has occurred, a transfer in which the traditional and proper wellsprings of power have been displaced by immoral or predatory special interests. Producers now support parasites. Whites suffer for the advancement of blacks. The sexually immoral threaten the moral integrity of the nation. Oligarchy threatens democracy. Parents have lost control of schools. Merit has been replaced by racial and ethnic favoritism. The heterosexual family is threatened by homosexual couples. The inversions of order and civility are cumulative. For many, these changes amount to an insidious revolution in manner and morals.

The despair is profound and the anger is heartfelt. The American Dream has lost much of its magic. But talk radio also has a vocal and substantial minority of patriotic and trusting voices for whom economic opportunity and social justice are very real.

Many people say—mostly Democrats—that minorities, Puerto Ricans, Chicanos, blacks, can't make it in America now. That native Americans who have been here for a long time have it sewed up, that they control the banks and big business and the stock market and that they keep these people out. Well this is a lot of bunk, there is no country in the world where poor people and minorities get so much help and where the law requires equal employment. You can still make it in America and make it big if you are willing to work and work hard. The opportunities are there, plenty of opportunities. Every day I read about some poor guy who made it—got an education and made it. This is a country were hard work pays off— a little education and hard work.

We got the highest standard of living in the world. People are moving from the slums to the suburbs all the time. They must have made it. So don't tell me there's no more opportunity in America. That's a lot of bunk. Sure the Rockefellers and other rich people have a lot of things sewed up, but, by God, there is plenty left for people who are willing to work and work hard. When I was a kid, I read some of those Horatio Alger stories. Well, much of those stories are still true. The trouble is that so many people get so much from the government—welfare and unemployment—that they don't want to work. They're better off not working. So they become parasites on the rest of us—lazy bums who do know you can still make it. The system isn't closed. Sure there are monopolies and there are places where minority people will probably never get in, but it's still the individual who counts.

I don't care what people say, free enterprise is still the best. Look at what happened to communist countries. The state is on everyone's back, not enough food, long lines in the stores, not enough refrigerators or anything else. These people are hard up. Our captialism has worked for most. We got a huge middle class and its getting bigger. We got plenty of food and goods. Our kids can make it if they are willing to work. There's plenty of state colleges with low tuition and plenty of education for poor boys to prepare them to make it. You still can't keep a poor kid down who got brains and guts. Free enterprise did this, still plenty of opportunity. Competition works, it does make people work hard to get rewards. And don't forget, we've got all those freedoms, too. Don't you think our freedoms are connected to free enterprise?

This reasoned defense of Horatio Alger and America's historical self-image, this moderate and reasonable fusion of reality and hope, is not the dominant theme of political talk radio, but much of it is consistent with the results of polls taken during the crisis of confidence. Despite the pervasive mistrust of big business and corporate self-interest, the overwhelming majority of Americans continue to believe in the virtues of free enterprise and competition. The mistrustful distinguish between the behavior of big business, of which they strongly disapprove, and the economic system, of which they strongly approve. It is as if big business, the core of the economy, were a separate and temporarily delinquent adjunct of the system that can be reprogrammed and return to society. We have noted that this ability to compartmentalize and isolate objects of mistrust permits Americans to vent their spleen and yet remain passonately committed to basic values. In a most peculiar way, mistrust becomes metaphysical. The liberal consensus can withstand very large explosions of mistrust because this safety value exists. The compulsive commitment to the liberal tradition creates the need for an escape valve, a mechanism that insures the purity of the system, a nationalism that holds free enterprise and electoral politics blameless.

Public opinion data cited earlier indicate that majorities of people believe that capitalism is a precondition for the maintenance and protection of basic freedoms and rights. Americans do not believe that such rights are possible in socialist or communist societies. Free enterprise is the core American idea. Free politics depends on its existence. The right to organize politically provides some with the hope that political remedies exist.

> **Prior to busing we stayed home and took care of our husbands. We no longer go to the voting booth and vote for a man because he has a nice sound. We research the issues. We know where they stand. We have become educated as to where the power is; the power of the media, the power of the politicians, the fact the race is not necessarily good and necessarily bad. We don't follow the party line. People are becoming involved in issues that affect themselves and their kids. We are not dumb. We know how you go about getting things done—it is a healthy thing for a democratic society.**

Some maintain their commitment to America by refusing to believe that the good image of the Republican Party has been tarnished.

> **I can't believe that Carter and the men around him [re: Bert Lance] are anything like Nixon. It's all too cynical. This criticism is all soap opera tactics. Who is sleeping with who. It's all distorted. The networks had to dramatize it to the hilt. These guys are out to make a buck and they will**

**distort the truth. This stuff about corruption is destroying
our good image of the government.**

Neoconservative mistrust is not likely to abate until the state curbs
its omnivorous desire for power and control—the rapaciousness that
perverts elected officials and bureaucrats. Bureaucracy feeds on itself. The demand is always for greater appropriations, more programs, more personnel, and more regulations. The threat to individual
free choice mounts. This domino theory leads to the view that a
clear and present danger exists: the threat is imminent. This danger
necessitates an immediate and large-scale counterattack. This is the
mood that Mr. Reagan understood. But neither he nor the opposition
understood that millions of Democrats and liberals, as well as conservatives, were disenchanted. The president prospered because mistrust was bipartisan.

Conservative callers and many liberals share a sense of urgency,
a sense that the destructive powers of the state have eroded so much
free choice, dispensed so much inequity that, if redemption is to
come, it must be swift and mighty. The destruction unleashed liberalism has much to do with the fact that the Democrats have forsaken
fact for theory, reality for abstraction. Presidents Kennedy, Johnson,
and Carter, in the opinion of conservatives and liberals, constructed
grand schemes of social reorganization based on abstract moral and
political principles—universals such as equality, justice, and affirmative action—abstractions that fail to take into account the highly
particular and unique problems and priorities of individuals. Individual differences, the nuances of particular need, are not amenable
to a public policy based on abstractions and aggregates. Only an
individual can make a best choice. Society is nothing but the sum
of individuals. Regulation by general principle inevitably damages
freedom.

This individualism is ironic because conservative thought is so
wedded to abstract pronouncement and universal principle (e.g.,
what's good for business is good for the country) that it overlooks
the contexts of class, power, and coercion that actually define what
exists and what might exist. The conservative world is a world of
free individuals who make voluntary choices. Every individual de-
termines his life chances, not the class system, or the stucture of

opportunity, or the matter of race. Opportunity in America is available to those who make the right choices; poverty is the result of poor life choices. Every man is responsible for his own life; no one is responsible for another. Society, the social structure, is an abstraction and not a vital force.

Liberal callers do not concur with most of this social theory, but hundreds of hours of talk radio make it clear that liberals are becoming more conservative and conservatives are becoming more reactionary. Democratic working men and women in large numbers oppose social welfare and affirmative action as much as Republicans. They, too, believe that welfare encourages people not to work and destroys character. They, too, believe that the system creates poverty and encourages fathers to abandon their families. They also expound a "reverse Marxism," in which the poor leech off the rich.

Because the crisis of confidence was bipartisan, and because the Democratic Party was in power during much of the 1960s and 1970s, it is not surprising that mistrust of America served the Republican cause in the 1980s. The mistrust of America, so evident in talk radio, was more profound and caustic than was reported by pollsters in the 1960s and 1970s. The political alienation was more pervasive and the commitment to the future more tenuous, perhaps because callers paid a great deal of to the degradation of state and local politics, an area unexplored by the chroniclers of the crisis. The debasement of everyday life, the lack of safety at night, the unreliability of the police, and other matters of extreme mistrust were not attended by pollsters. The crisis of confidence was not restricted to national politics, big business, and the professions. More significant than the profound mistrust of state and local politics, was the sense that the exchanges of daily life—the most intimate aspects of living—had become corroded.

The estrangement was moral and spiritual, as well as political. The crisis, for many, was a response to the decay of civic virtue and to the shattering of communal bonds, those reciprocal ties of mutual aid and comfort that mute self-interest and make a general will feasible. If we interpret callers correctly, their lack of confidence is an expression of their desire to redefine the meaning of a moral and productive life. The crisis was cultural as well as political and economic.

For many, the moral crisis was epitomized by the curtailment of freedom and the erosion of self-reliance by an omnivorous and incompetent state. The work ethic and the strength of character potentiated by that ethic are casualties of this spiritual crisis.

There are, in fact, two crises. Liberals believe that the ethical and legal restraints on self-interest that are necessary for the production of a common good have been emasculated. Unmitigated self-interest is promoting manipulation rather than productivity, damaging civic virtue, and distorting human nature. Individual license is negating social need. Private right is frustrating the public good. This is ironic because it was the liberal Democrats in the Kennedy and Johnson administrations who perfected interest-group politics, with its emphasis on private and group self-interest. The practitioners of particularism now believe that particularism is the root cause of the crisis.

There is a second crisis of confidence, a neoconservative mistrust, founded on quite different concerns. Conservatives are concerned with the state's attack on self-reliance and freedom of choice. Self-interest, self-reliance, and freedom of choice are the ultimate neoconservative virtues, the fulcrum around which character develops. Freedom of choice is the critical freedom, and egoism is the only mode through which that freedom may be achieved. The crisis of confidence was created when the state began to violate the free development of individuality.

The state cheapens the individual, degrades the work ethic, rewards the deviant and incompetent, punishes virtue, creates poverty, erodes discipline, and ultimately destroys the delicate organic relationship between individuals and groups necessary for the generation of civic virtue and economic growth. The state also forces individuals to behave immorally, because they must develop abnormal strategies to survive in a nation characterized by artificial and immoral state contrivances. The crisis of confidence is perceived as a conflict of two cultures: the culture of politics and business, and the culture of a free people.

The culture of politics and business is amoral, corrupt, and self-serving; it thrives on collusion and immunity. The popular culture, the culture of everyday life, is bound by traditional moral prescription and the belief that honesty, self-reliance, and hard work are

meaningful. The culture of power confronts its increasingly powerless counterpart.

Periodically, an individual caller, more thoughtful and articulate
than most, beautifully illuminates the crisis of confidence. The callers
who perform this service most eloquently often take the prosaic
interchanges of daily life—greeting, behavior in traffic, an enounter
with a policeman—a construct from them a diagnosis of civic life.

4

Have A Nice Day

T HE essential character of nations is often revealed in the seemingly petty habits of daily life, the amenities and routines of
everyday existence by which people civilize or brutalize each other.
The alienated, who populate political talk radio, repeatedly cite the
failure of people to say good morning or thank you, the failure to
return a cafeteria tray, and the failure to offer a seat to an older
person. They decry children's lack of respect for parents, teenage
sex, and the aggressiveness of drivers. They are preoccupied with
the disappearance of what they call good manners and civil behavior.
They fear to walk on the public streets. The more sophisticated
among them relate this decline to the norms of those who govern:
Nixon, Agnew, and the Watergate plumbers are, for them, proto-
typical. Watergate is a symbol of higher immorality. The alienated
voter, a reservist in the army of the discontented in the 1960s and
1970s, is most visible in his favorite preserve, the radio talk show,
which became a repository of civic complaints during the crisis of
confidence.

The talk shows of 1977 were dominated by hatred of "forced
busing," of Democratic social programs, of politicians, of big business, and of the judiciary. "Forced busing" was perceived as reverse
racism, which would produce, as one citizen put it, "nigger control
of the schools." Welfare was perceived as a boon to "blacks, parasites,
and bums." Callers, particularly those in the lower middle class,
feared that neighborhood life and real estate values would disintegrate
with the end of school segregation. They were frightened that paying
the taxes necessary for the "preferential" treatment of the poor and
blacks would threaten their economic status, already tenuous at best.

Almost daily, callers exuded racist sentiment and a brooding sense that the government of the United States had lost touch with its historic commitment to white supremacy.

Five years later, talk radio was preoccupied with the depletion of the moral and spiritual resources of city people—the loss of the manners and morals that make for civil life. When callers spoke of urban disarray, they cited unemployment and escalation of black crime, discourtesy on buses, cheating by Medicare physicians, the need for double locks, and the fact that licenses, tax abatements, and permits of all kinds are for sale by the city or state. For Catholic callers, the disintegration of urban life had an ultimate cause: abortion and the break-up of the family.

The prime civic complaint was political corruption in the cities in the state, and in the nation. The pervasive debasement of public life was perceived as a cancer on the body politic that affects the conduct of campaigns, voting, and the determination of public policy.

Busing was largely forgotten. The great majority of callers saw it as a failure that exacerbated racism and ruined the schools. Talk of the high cost of social welfare programs was muted. Talk of welfare chiselers, the constituency of bleeding-heart liberals, was rarely heard and then primarily on the conservative show. Corruption, oligarchy, nepotism, and civic disorder were the order of the day.

The response of many to this civic disorder was harsh: the demand was for punishment and more punishment. The agenda for the early 1980s was mandatory sentencing, the death penalty, the elimination of state funding for abortion, and cuts in spending for social programs. The mood was punitive and uncharitable. Though a New Deal Democrat was elected governor of Massachusetts in 1982, support for New Deal programs among working people who phoned was small. Inflation and the stereotype of incumbents as crooks produced victories for liberal challengers in Massachusetts, but not a humane predisposition or a commitment to liberalism. The talk show was full of adversarial feeling and anger.

Five days a week, the callers called, the host responded, and the civic complaints mounted. Months of listening leave the impression that a vast underground of discontent and anger lies below the surface of American life. This underground appears rarely in the national press or on television, perhaps because it is an embarrassment. On occasion, the networks document alienated Americans, but the presentation creates the impression that they are a quaint minority of malcontents, eccentrics who are of interest primarily because they illustrate, by contrast, how content is the remainder of the nation.

Talk radio, as we have noted, is much more chaotic, undirected, and discursive than the data gathered by pollsters; but it is much richer, more detailed, and revealing. This verbatim register of feeling is often structured by the host, who can terminate callers, alter topics, bait, cajole, and force the issue. The host's ideology is the fixed star around which the talk gravitates.

Avi Nelson, the son of a rabbi, is a thoughtful neoconservative and a highly skilled talk show host; he is deeply committed to the virtues of pure capitalism and the Protestant ethic. He was educated at Yale, did graduate work at Harvard, and learned his lessons from the classic texts of European and American conservatism. He skillfully dissects callers who oppose the conservative gospel, exposing their "faulty" logic, dismissing their data, and criticizing their theories. At the same time, he presents a doomsday history of liberal public policy, which commences with the election of Franklin Roosevelt, the event that marked America's fall from grace, and extends through the misguided and counterproductive follies of affirmative action, forced busing and welfare.

The fixed star of Nelson's ideological firmament is liberty, the absolute freedom of individual choice. His perspective is Social Darwinian. His mythic ego ideal is Horatio Alger and his "compleat" economist is Milton Friedman. Competition and the struggle for existence, unhindered by the state, are the twin highways to economic expansion and personal freedom. Listeners to *The Avi Nelson Show* are offered a melange of classical and neoconservative doctrine—Adam Smith, Arthur Laffer, and Edward Teller—which is intended to reaffirm the virtues of laissez faire, self-reliance, capital accumulation, and the trickle-down effect. To Avi Nelson, and most who phone WITS, Boston, supply-side economics and the curtailment of social welfare is the true faith, consonant with the Founding Fathers' intention to create a free nation based on individual initiative and private property.

Nelson promises triumph and redemption. He shares the populist dream that the good sense of the common man will prevail over the mad and unpragmatic abstractions of the liberal intelligentsia. The American people will become painfully aware of liberal follies. The high cost of public beneficience and the pitiful return will be reflected in tax increases, while tampering with immutable economic and social laws will cause stagflation. Liberal indulgence will extract a price so great and so painful that harsh reality will free popular consciousness from the follies of the Democratic Party. Liberalism will then fall of its own weight.

Conservatism will triumph because liberals have neither charismatic heroes nor a relevant political philosophy. The leader of liberal villainy Edward Kennedy, is no longer legitimate: his sexual peccadilloes have tarnished the myth of Camelot. The liberals have no heroes, no Holy Grail, no quest, no Galahad. The Democrats are moribund. The good memory of the party's past has been replaced by an image of Carter's ineptitude. For Avi Nelson and his callers, the triumph of conservatism is a matter of time, a matter of patience.

Conservative talk radio is cast as a melodrama, replete with heroes, knaves, fools, conspiracies, and saviors. Nelson's history of the United States is based on the assumption that the republic was a land of virtue and just reward for much of its existence. The nation had a golden age, characterized by pure capitalism and the Protestant ethic, a productive epoch in which "everyman" gave an hour's work for an hour's pay, and in which men still lived within a moral system that defined good and evil. The golden age was the age of Horatio Alger, the age of church, family, and labor, the age of respect for law and placid order. It was also an age of military power and Manifest Destiny: America was not afraid to protect its liberal truth in the nineteenth century by enforcing the Monroe Doctrine or using military force. The golden age of American history was the period when William Graham Sumner was a prophet and Coolidge and Hoover were wise enough to do nothing.

Franklin Delano Roosevelt and John Maynard Keynes destroyed this state of nature. Government regulation of the economy violated Adam Smith's first principle, while social programs for the underclass violated the law of survival of the fittest. The halcyon age gave way to crime in the streets, welfare chiselers, and recurrent recession. But the fall from grace inevitably produces redemption. Faith in America is the theme of this drama. The spirit of laissez-faire and the invention of supply-side economics will restore the golden age. Americans will return to their proper place in the world and unrestrained capitalism will restore the morality of rugged individualism.

Jerry Williams, the liberal host, is a committed New Dealer, a muckraker in the classic tradition, who relentlessly scrutinizes the alleged corruption of state and local politics, while reminding his listeners that their political alienation is well founded. The state is essentially an oligarchy that tenaciously protects the interests of its business affiliates, and that masks its true purpose through the judicial dispensation of largesse to the underclass. This benediction creates the illusion of social justice, legitimizes the state, and pacifies much of the public.

The very rich own America; of this, there is no doubt. American politics—particularly state and local politics—represents a network of competing self-interests that appears to satisfy democratic requisites but that often sacrifices the general welfare to the needs of the corporate rich and political elite. The political system has prospered for so long on the principle of quid pro quo and particularism that amoral pragmatism has displaced law and equity as a public standard. Self-interest and corruption, sanctified by the passage of time, have lost much of their moral stigma.

Williams's views may be related to the fact that he grew up in the unique Jewish culture of New York City, where Talmudic righteousness and European socialism flourished until the Jews were Americanized and Franklin Roosevelt's compassion muted Jewish exceptionalism. The Jews, even when denuded of socialist feeling, maintained a sense of righteous indignation and social justice that led them to believe that American labor, despite its affluence, remained a prime source of power to be exploited. Williams's political scenario remains basically an expression of that Jewish ghetto outlook: good constantly overwhelmed by evil, labor constantly abused by capitalism, the citizen constantly debased by the state. This scenario is a natural for talk radio. Listeners are excited by the controversy and anger, the confrontation of good and evil, the vindication of the alienated voter.

The liberal drama, like its conservative counterpart, centers on the struggle between good and evil, but for Boston callers the drama is largely staged in Boston and Massachusetts. The actors are state and local politicians, contractors, builders, real estate developers, bankers, insurance companies, and defeated office holders and their relatives who plunder the public from City Hall and the State House. The leading roles are played by the mayor of Boston and his henchmen, and the legislative elite. Their methods of operation, the motif of the liberal drama, are nepotism and graft.

The political culture of Massachusetts and Boston, in Williams's view, resembles that of the 1890s: a world of the city boss and his machine, of midnight judges, ethnic politics, uncontested and inflated contracts, padded expenses, pay-offs, kickbacks, cronyism, and Medicean family loyalties. The sisters, brothers, and friends, and former colleagues of politicians fill the public payroll, occupy posts on licensing boards, and fall into obscurity only to reappear with a Cadillac and a new house.

The leitmotif of this political drama is the decay of democracy and the triumph of special interests. The victims are the alienated voter and the public interest. The democratic body politic has been decimated by sleazy professionals and lobbyists who feed on the public carcass. The result for Williams and his callers is "Taxachusetts."

There is a pathos about the liberal talk show. Jerry Williams speaks of the Democrats as if intellectual hardening of the arteries set in with the death of Franklin Roosevelt. He asks liberal guests and callers for new solutions, fresh approaches, but none are forthcoming. Mondale suggests nothing unknown to Kennedy and Johnson. Democrats are unable to deal with the bureaucratic problems and inequities created by the welfare state, or with the related problems of race and special privilege. Jerry Williams and his guests are really talking about the atrophy of liberalism and the failure to create a civic culture of trust and responsibility.

The quality of civic culture became the topic of Williams talk show during the summer of 1982, when the Brookings Institution published a lengthy study of fifty-three American cities in decline. Boston was cited among the five most troubled cities. Within a few days after the Brookings report was published, another study concluded that half of the residents of Massachusetts wished to leave the Commonwealth. The liberal host seized the topic and devoted an entire program to the issue of whether one wished to leave the Bay State or remain. An unusually well-spoken man (who later identified himself as a historian) responded. He was prompted to call because the host had terminated a young caller earlier in the program with the epithet, "You're stupid, you're really stupid." The historian, offended by this invective, attempted, in the tradition of Tocqueville, to capture the essence of culture through scrutiny of the most ordinary acts and speech of everyday life: how people greet one another, how they drive, the language they use, the hostility of their financial dealings, their skepticism and fear of warm personal relations, and the nature of the masks they wear. The historian commences.

I am originally from Washington, D.C., and come up here for the summers for two years now and I was listening to your program. I come to Cape Cod, and I've considered a few times moving up, and frankly one of the things I have the most difficulty with is the lack of kindness and openness of the people. And I was only moved to call you after the remark you made to the young boy about being stupid. That was sort of the epitome to me of what I find in Massachusetts and what I have not found in other places I have lived.

I was only joking.

I know, but that was on the air and it was in public. And there was a young man who called up proudly to say something . . . and he is probably hurt. That is lack of real friendliness. It is the kind of conversation I find myself engaging in, rather than a smile, warmth, and that sort of thing.

Do you find that on the Cape?

I found it in the Boston area and on the Cape. I found it everywhere I've been here, yes.

The host is in the business of criticizing Massachusetts politics and society day after day. His constituency is the army of the alienated and his appeal, in part, is based on developing a resonance with the discontented. But there are limits to which the fatherland can be humiliated; the acerbic joke can be overplayed. He senses that he is dealing with an unusual adversary—forceful, but not strident, so he raises the banner of the Bay State.

I don't find that necessarily to be so. I might do a little number like that on somebody on the air, but it is essen-

tially only done in jest and fun. I don't find that necessarily
to be so. I think that once you're implanted here for three
to six months, you'll find everybody to be fairly warm and
friendly and kind.

The caller will not be deterred.

My wife is originally from the Cape and one of the reasons
she left was that she found . . . she finally found that it
was getting to her. She moved away and has been away
except for these summers with me. You may be right. On
the other hand, I would answer that by saying perhaps
you've just gotten used to this gross behavior.

[The host agrees.]

As I say, there's a conditioning process that sets in here
when you live in Greater Boston and you're trying to drive
an automobile, you finally get used to the idea that everybody's an idiot.

Well, that's a good metaphor as well. I mean that it does
extend to the roads and I have lived in California and spent
some time in L.A., and that sort of thing, and again I find
horrible traffic situations in which people back off and let
you in, and look around and try to see what the most
convenient thing is for everyone, rather than basically I
feel like I'm taking my life in my hands on the highway
in Massachusetts.

It's a way of life, everyone out there is shifting for themselves. Aggrandizement on the road is a normal way of
life in Boston, and when it became that way, the abnormal
and dangerous became normal. Everybody expects to be
killed. It's become our way of life here all throughout
Massachusetts because obviously Boston is the leader and
everybody follows our lead.

Well again, I would see it as a sort of metaphor for a
larger sort of an approach to other people and I guess

that's what you're saying, but I find it very uncomfortable, and as much as I like snowy winters and I certainly enjoy the summers here, but as much as I enjoy many of the things about them, I really, really don't want to spend much time around most of the people I've met.

The host, on the defensive, asks, "Well, would it be any different in Washington?" The answer surprises him because he assumes that Massachusetts manners and mores are universal.

Yes, very different. I was in Virginia for about ten years before that, and of course, that's a *very* different sort of world, which I gather New Englanders often find superficial. Your Northeastern gruffness is so entrenched and taken as so normal, taken as the normal state of man's relations, that an exception—kindness and courtesy—must be a ploy. And they feel people are being phoney when they're that nice and that sort of thing. And coming from California, I thought the same myself. But I very quickly realized that it may be a ritual people go through, but it is a heartfelt ritual. And the gentleness, the friendliness, the warmth people greet you with rubs off into a whole sort of lifestyle and makes it more pleasant to deal, obviously, with your family and close friends—one is going to be kind and nice and that sort of thing—but in your daily contacts on the road or in the store or whatever, in California, Virginia, Washington, D.C., for example—the three places I know pretty well and West Virginia for one year—all four of these places are all places where I feel more comfortable stepping out into the world.

The gentleness and intelligence of this caller unnerve the host because he refuses to universalize Massachusetts manners and morals. For the historian, Massachusetts is an exception, a debasement. For his host, the Bay State is prototypically American.

Mocking his caller's description of West Virginia, the host cynically asks, "Well, how many times can you hear somebody say, 'Have a nice day?' " "Um, it makes a difference." "I don't know if it makes a difference or not. I think people are a little more real around here."

Well, that's what I was saying about people from New England thinking that's phony. There's an internal process that goes on, whereby when one is nice, one becomes nice, and the whole world is nicer in general, and I have talked to some relatives here and people I've talked to— and they obviously have no idea what I'm talking about, about having the world be a kinder place but I really think (nervous laugh) you all are missing something up here by no backing off a little and being a little kinder to each other.

Well, I don't necessarily agree with that point of view, I think we have in Massachussetts tough politics, a harder life than those that are down in the warmer areas of the world, our taxes are much higher than they are in the state of Virginia and the state of Maryland. We have tough politics, very tough winters, as a matter of fact, and I think it maybe puts a facade around New Englanders or Bostonians, but once here it's more colorful. We're not all painted with the bland anemic stereotype.

The caller is annoyed, "I don't call it bland. I don't call it bland at all. It's very colorful."

No, but what I'm saying is that if you were to come into Boston and were to go into one neighborhood, like the North End, you'll never find the North End in Washington, D.C. I mean, we have colorful neighborhoods, exciting and different kinds of people, from various places, a good blend, mix of ethnic groups. When I was in Washington for just a short period of time, a few months, I didn't find anything very exciting there.

I'm not arguing excitement. I'm arguing . . . I'm not saying one place is better than another. I'm talking about quality, a characteristic that I really . . . I understand the business about the hard winters and, I'm a historian, so I look at things in that sort of perspective. I understand what you're saying about the psychological impact of dirty politics and that sort of thing, but to me, that's all the more reason to frankly sort of back off and let your, let the other parts of your life take a deep breath every now and then and let things be a little gentle. I don't understand . . . I don't understand people going with so much, rather than trying to overcome what seems to me to be a real hostility and harshness in interpersonal relationships. It seems to me that that would be the place to back off maybe . . . there's more reason to be kind in your small interactions here than there is in Virginia, because Virginia is warmer and more . . . easier place to get along and that sort of thing. Do you see what I'm saying?

I understand what you're saying but I don't think it's necessarily so. You might find when you were down in the market place on Friday, down in Boston, that some guy was a little gruff with you over the fact that you handled a peach or a tomato and he wanted to get one from the bottom of the pack. Well, that's part of the game and underneath that crusty exterior lives a heart of gold.

I understand. Obviously, the family pulls together. People have these fine relationships. No, no, I won't argue with you on any of that. I do contend, however that that gruff exterior is not necessary and that it feeds on itself in such a way and I find with some in-laws I have up here—we've talked about this at length—and I think that they have intellectually understood what I've said about showing more positive feelings rather than that gruff exterior and the impact it can have on the internal picture. When the world is battering at you, you've got to put up strengths, and facades, and walls, and then it takes a long time to bring them down, and it seems to me so silly to put them up at all.

The historian has made his argument. The host seems no longer able to cope. He concludes the discussion with a display of old New

England hospitality, "Well, if you come to Massachusetts, if you decide to come to Massachusetts, I'm going to take you around for— this is an open invitation—to show you how kind and friendly we can be. I'm going to take you on an open invitation and introduce you in one full day to a lot of warm and friendly people." "Well, I'll call you on that." With this agreement, the host bids the historian, "Good luck and thanks for calling."

The difference in perspective between the critic and his host was provoked when the latter told the young caller that he was stupid. This confirmed the historian's belief that the hostile jibe is the lingua franca of Massachusetts. The historian understands that the debasement of common courtesy reflects a highly competitive economy and a harsh climate; he realizes that discourtesy and aggressiveness are functionally appropriate defenses against a competitive environment. He understands that the protocols of daily life are derivative and not autonomous. He does not argue, however—as Marxists would— that a change in manners and morals depends upon a change in economic structure. He merely suggests that Massachusetts people "are missing something by not backing off a little," although he shrewdly notes that the harshness of life, the winters, the dirty politics are "all the more reason to frankly sort of back off and let . . . the other parts of your life take a deep breath every now and then and let things be a little gentle."

He insists that manners profoundly affect the way life is lived. For him, values, and codes of conduct intimately influence daily life and economic relations. They exert an independent and powerful effect on social relations and they are not necessarily derivative of the economy. Los Angeles is as competitive as Boston and yet "people do back off." The crisis of confidence is, for him, a crisis of incivility.

This crisis of incivility was known to the pollsters who recorded the crisis of confidence. They reported that very large numbers of respondents believed that selfishness is the prime cause of the crisis of confidence. The crisis has much to do with the disintegration of the codes governing civil behavior. This disintegration of manners and morals reflected and contributed to the social and political pathology of the 1960s and 1970s.

Ths historian understands the larger meaning of this incivility. Enmity and indifference feed upon themselves, infect the body politic, and ultimately drive away good sentiment. The war of all against all becomes the most natural system of mutual defense.

The hostility engendered by the harshness of Massachusetts politics, the hard winters, the intense competition, and the racism, once set in motion, reciprocates; that is why it must be curbed as soon as possible. One kind word sets others in motion. It is an ancient and simple message, a variation on Christian themes and Kant's categorical imperative.

Social relations in the Bay State have become treacherous because malice and estrangements in daily life are taken as normal. Hostility has become the norm.

The put-down, for example, is taken by the host as a perfectly normal, perfectly acceptable humorous device. The hostile wisecrack has been the language of the Boston streets for so long that little stigma is attached to it. In the process, the language of civility has become a second language. Mores change slowly, and the change is rarely noticed. The debasement of everyday life, so spectacular and disquieting to the alien, is standard operating procedure to the citizens of Boston. The historian tells the host that he does not realize what he is doing because "you've gotten used to" it. The host admits this, and excuses himself. "There's a conditioning process that sets in here when you live in Greater Boston and you're trying to drive an automobile, you finally get used to the idea that everybody's an idiot." The more one perceives other drivers as idiots, the more courtesy on the road and safety will be threatened. The devolution of public decency and the elevation of public sentiment are gravitational: they accelerate unless met by an opposing force. The crisis of confidence is that acceleration.

But courtesy breeds more civil behavior. The caller cites Los Angeles, where tradition of courtesy on the road bred more courtesy.

The historian is sensitive to the wider meaning of aggressive driving. "I would see it [driving] as a sort of metaphor for a larger sort of an approach to other people." The smallest aspects of daily life—the way people drive, or greet one another, or wait in line—are both a reflection of their alienation and a cause of its exacerbation.

The caller assumes that New Englanders, jaded as they are, would take the courtliness of Virginians to be phony, but he insists that common courtesy performs a most significant social function.

The greeting of the 1970s, "Have a nice day," may be a saccharine and hollow ritual for the host, but for the guest, "it makes a difference." Social amenities produce and reproduce the warm context that nourishes life.

The rituals of courtliness would be dysfunctional in Massachusetts because contentiousness is the appropriate medium of interaction. "People are a little more real around here. In Massachusetts, the experience is hard nose struggle." The host is so much a product of the Darwinian struggle for existence that he perceives not only the manners and mores of Virginia as unreal, but the way of life itself. Virginia, with its "Have a nice day," represents a more primitive and archaic America. And surely this is the historian's point. It has become impossible—given the value placed on self-interest and the competition it nourishes—to conceive of a kinder world.

The host and the historian perceive the world so differently that they can no longer communicate. The host is so perfectly socialized that he assumes that local mores are universal; the critic conceives of a better social life. The host, a loyal patriot, assumes it exists: that the local way of life *is* the better way.

The historian's affirmation of courtesy and kindness is traditionally American. It contains little that is shocking or radical—merely a request for thoughtfulness. But the criticism of poor manners is actually a statement about the nature of the social contract. The crassness of daily life reflects the dissolution of common bonds, the debilitation of community spirit, the sense that people are no longer engaged in a common enterprise or bound together for the general good. The critic assumes that egoism shatters the commune and produces an aggrandizing manner that contaminates social relations. The decline of common courtesy follows the decline of common purpose. People draw apart, separated by antagonistic aims. Skepticism and hostility become appropriate adaptive responses. This is the ultimate crisis of confidence, reflected in politics, big business, and labor, and prismatically illustrated in the interchanges of everyday life.

The historian was a sensitive caller, acutely tuned to the nuances of manner and language. His talk enriched the show, and provided it with a depth and sensibility, an urgency and seriousness, that radio talk achieves only on occasion. Many callers—less articulate, but equally alienated—addressed the issue of leaving or remaining in Massachusetts. They were preoccupied with the dangers of the city, the filth of public transportation, and the corruption of the police; they were preoccupied with the dissolution of civil life.

People who are afraid to ride on the Orange Line can always take the competing rapid transit system, of which there is none. The second thing is we could do it the South African way, we could segregate one car for whites only and the rest for anyone who wants to get on. And the reasonable thing that would never be done is that we could segregate one car out of four as a security car. You pay twice the fare, and there'd be someone there to profect you, a cop or a security guard.

The fear of public transportation naturally leads callers to discuss the other dangers of urban life—mugging in particular.

You can go out at night, but I don't dare. The streets are full of wild kids who would steal your teeth for a dime, or your coat, or your car. Dope, they need money for dope. So they steal and mug. I'm sixty-three years old. What am I going to do if someone grabs me? The city doesn't give a damn about protecting poor people. Streetlights are broken. You never see a cop. And if you did, it wouldn't do any good. The city is dangerous and filthy. If I could leave, I would.

But you go down to the fancy shopping centers—Copley Place, Faneuil Hall, and you find plenty of light and plenty of cops, or Beacon Hill where the rich live, plenty of light, plenty of cops. Isn't that what the city is all about—big business and big people.

I live in a less-fashionable part of town. We're right near the Brighton line, and if we need a service or anything cleaned up or taken care of, it's almost impossible to get the town to do it. Yet you drive down the more affluent, wealthier areas, everything is kept beautifully. That's extremely frustrating. It gives you the feeling that the city is only interested in rich people and the rich people can get what they want. I'm beginning to wonder why I vote. It doesn't seem to do me any good. Money is what counts.

The subject of mugging and poor municipal services excites a chorus of callers with essentially the same refrain: danger in the streets, poor lighting, unreliable police, fear, desperate blacks, and drugs. Most callers are profoundly alienated and find urban life fearsome and lonely. They make little effort to appreciate or understand the plight of the city. They are interested in crime and severe punishment. Occasionally the strident civic complaint is interrupted by a compassionate and unracist voice, but that voice is soon drowned out by the harsh—indeed, brutal—demand for retribution.

Forty-four percent of the arrests for crimes in Boston were blacks, they committed apparently forty-four percent of the crimes, and make up a minority of the population. The facts don't exclude white people, but there seems to be a tendency for violence and crime, especially by young black men. There are all sorts of horrible solutions to this that I won't go into now. In terms of drugs, drugs as I see it are being taken by youth out of desperation. We have an issue of unemployment that is extremely high among minority youth or youth in general—and if that is the case, then you don't have any other means of doing anything, so consequently they're just hanging out on the streets, and they're prone to all kinds of things that are going to get them in trouble.

If you lived where I do, you wouldn't say such things. Black people go to school, they can get an education, and they can get jobs. There's nothing holding them back. Plenty of opportunity. And where are they, taking drugs, robbing, vandalism, or welfare, having babies, fathers gone. They've become animals, bums, crooks. There's unemployment for white kids too. They all have it tough, but do you see them drunk and running through the streets? No, I don't care what you say, they are different. It's their own fault, but they are different. I'm sick of all this special treatment. It doesn't do any good. It wastes money. What we need is more cops and more harsh laws. Then you won't get so much trouble. By the way, some of them do make it, so that proves they could do it if they wanted to.

But many callers do not believe that more police would be effective. The urban world has been inverted. The policeman has become the law, not its servant—another example of the crisis who uses his public position to feed private gain.

The police feel that they are totally above the law. They can abuse people and when they do, it's okay. The rest of us do something and it's totally different. Let's not kid each other. The police have stake in certain types of crime— bookies, pimps, dope. Crime which needs protection. The cops know where most of these guys are, but they don't want to close them down. They would rather get paid off. And this is related to all these people who call about getting mugged. They are right. The cops don't care, they are too busy in more-profitable parts of the city—not all— many.

The issue of police protection and civic order, a central element of Boston's crisis of confidence, came to a head in 1982, when policemen allegedly killed a patron in a barroom brawl and badly injured others. The topic proccupied political talk radio for several days.

Jesus, it's terrible this is what causes these things to happen in this life, and you can see it, it's written all over them how they [police] act, they're so damned prima donna-ish, it's terrible, with that badge on someone really has to cut them down to size.

I live in Everett, and I've lived in Everett all my life. I've called those palookas up there to tell them what the hell is going on. It seems to me this whole city from the mayor

down should be thrown the hell out. I'm only one of many
that feel the same way in Everett, but what the hell can
people like us do? We vote and pay our taxes, and we
have a corrupt city police. They say only a few, but it's a
hell of a lot more than a few. I'm ashamed this is going
on in this city.

He got his head caved in by some unprofessional brutes
who were acting under the authority of law and I think
today we finally saw that because the spotlight is on. We
got indictments, and the whole city of Everett should
breathe a little easier. . . . I've seen them [police] do their
duty. I've seen my brother with a head that looked like a
broken watermelon, and if that's their duty then maybe
someone should do some duty to them.

The critics of Massachusetts culture argue that corruption has
become so commonplace and gone on for so long that it has become
the accepted way. One caller suggested that the police were a case
in point.

They [police] have been getting away with so much for
so long that they just think that they got the right to go
out and bully people. Just take things in their own hands,
and just think that they're the authority no matter what.

The alienated callers are groping to describe a view of public life
in which there are two political cultures, two rules of conduct, and
two distinct moral and legal systems. Like the respondents who were
polled during the crisis of confidence, they structure the political
world in terms of power and powerlessness, exploiters and exploited.
They have little doubt that the police and the state comprise a separate political culture, one that is immune from the legal restraints
and the morality that bind the masses. The alienated are developing
some sense of class consciousness, but it is primitive. They clearly
distinguish rich and poor, and they believe that the city exists primarily to serve the rich—that it exists "for big business and big
people." They realize that public services are distributed according
to wealth and that city government is much more responsive to the

rich. The less affluent know they are shortchanged. Their political efficacy is low; and voting appears to be a futile act.

But the callers do not seek the cause of this maldistribution of services, wealth, and power. No one suggests that distribution of urban justice has anything to do with the pattern of property ownership. Nothing is rooted in the economy. There is little sense of class, no sense of class conflict, and only a vague sense of exploitation. There is no coherent demand for social change and no idea of what kind of change might rectify the situation. The public mood is angry but passive, informed in some brute way but without sophistication.

But the elements of a political posture are developing: a fairly realistic posture that could become the basis for more radical action. Many callers correctly identify the sources of urban and state power. They correctly understand that two cultures exist, two sets of morals, two interpretations of justice, and two prescriptions for enforcing the law: one for the rich, another for the poor; one for the politically powerful, and one for the powerless.

They assume, with some justice, that the activities of the powerful are shrouded in secrecy and that revelations of wrongdoing are always incomplete. The idea of two cultures, two quite different worlds, could be the precursor of a more sophisticated approach.

These politicians and contractors and real estate operators and City Hall hangers on—they live in their own world. Got their own rules. They got their own law, their own morals—not like us. We do something wrong, the law gets us. We cheat, our customers leave and we get a bad name. They steal. They appoint cousins and aunts to state and city jobs—some jobs don't even exist—and they don't even get caught. There are two laws. One for us and one for them. They live in a different world. It's a world made to order, a world where things are done in secret. Where your buddies cover up. Those guys enter the State House— poor young kids—Irish, Italians, and now black—and in five years they are driving a Lincoln and live in a good place. Where do they get it? As if I didn't know. Selling favors, selling licenses, pocketing campaign contributions, that's where they get it. And nobody ever says a word. Once in a while, one of them gets it—indicted, convicted—what do you call it—a sacrificial lamb. Baloney, it's the tip of the iceberg. And, do you think they're any better in Washington? The stakes are bigger, that's the difference, that's all. It's everywhere, their world and ours.

It's not just the real estate tax, it's everything, if I stop at McDonalds to get a hamburger, I've got to kick out six cents on this tax or that. If I go to the store to buy almost anything except the food that I put on the table I gotta pay a tax on it. I sit down and I listen to people talk about taxes or read it in the paper I get so depressed, that I just keep saying to myself, "when the hell is all this going to end?" I live in this house, and I happen to love the home that I live in. My wife and I, we really—it's the one thing that we want in our lifetime, to have and own this home, and you wonder, if you're going to be able to keep it. You know I'd like to be able to die here, but I don't think I'm going to be able to die here, I think I'm going to die from taxation.

The thing that really bothers me most of all is that I can't understand how any person who works in the state legislature and makes $16,000–$60,000 a year can relate to my problem and my situation. I say they ought to take these judges and give them $8,000 a year and let them legislate, and see what they can do for us. They cannot, they just cannot represent me, they can't relate to me, they have no idea how depressing it is to try and get by on a lousy $8,000 a year. They live in a different world, a world we pay for.

The wider issue is urban pathology. There is more talk of mugging. "I don't go out after four o'clock at night. I'm afraid to walk anywhere. I never was afrair to walk in San Diego, but I'm afraid here." The liberal host affirms this female caller's view and speaks of the retreat of older people to Florida "to their little cubicles."

Well, in my year in Florida, by the way, I'd hear that all the time from people in Florida saying the same thing to me. Older folks who were saying, "we're afraid to go out at night." And I'd say, "where do you live?" And they'd say, "somewhere in Pompano Beach," which is just above Fort Lauderdale. I'd say, "well, why are you afraid to go out?" You see, their perception was that there was somebody going to get them even though there was nobody going to get them. Their perception was that they had to stay in so everybody's sort of locked into these little cubicles even in Florida, where, by the way, they have gone to escape, you know, the same thing you're looking to escape yourself. . . . I find that it's a perception. Yes, there are people who are mugged. There are people who are obviously dealt with in street crime, but it's not everybody. But what we see and hear obviously contributes to our attitudes. In Florida some of the older folks down there will not go out at night. . . . They call Collins Avenue in Miami Beach the world's largest bowling alley. Nobody out there at night.

The reality of crime in the streets may be substantially less than the fear of crime, but the fantasy has force and meaning of its own. The scenario is not unlike a surrealist film: elderly people huddled in cubicles, waiting for some unseen monster; formerly crowded and fashionable boulevards, meccas of consumerism, now deserted. The drama seems unreal, laced with fantasy, but it is very real to the actors. And it is Collins Avenue at night. The evening promenade, a traditional aspect of urban pleasure and civility, is gone.

The host reminds his listeners that the topic of the day is whether one plans to remain in the Bay State or leave.

The overture of the first male caller is brief. "I'm leaving." This classic alienated voter cites a litany of indictments and convictions of Massachusetts office holders and concludes with the popular sentiment, "for everyone that's caught, ten more should have been." "Hello, I'm leaving." "You're going. Where are you going?" "Out of Massachusetts." "Where to?" "North, where they have class." The host laughs, the caller begins to make his point.

Where you can wake up and you're not getting robbed and your politicians are not robbin' ya. The politicians here

on both sides of the fence—Republicans and Democrats—
I remember since I was a kid—Dow the sheriff in 1936,
went to jail. The mayor of Cambridge, Lyons, went to jail.
The same pattern is still going on and on and on. Corruption, corruption, corruption, and we're paying through
the nose. There's no end to it, no end.

You sound like you've been around Massachusetts for a
long time.

Yeah, a long time. I've been out and came back. I went
to Michigan. And that is just as bad.

And you're next heading to New Hampshire.

No, Vermont.

That's really a rural existence, though, it really is.

No, not anymore. I lived there for four years when I was
a young boy and look at Mt. Snow now. Who ever thought
it would be like that now. I'm going to tell you something.
There's no corruption up there like there is here. You leave
your door open at night. . . . Nothing like this. You're
afraid to speak to anyone here anymore. They're liable to
rob you. If your hair's got a little gray in it or it's snow
white, forget it, you're gone. Fortunately, I'm a big guy.
I'm six feet seven and I weigh 300 pounds. Nobody will
touch me even though my hair's snow white. You follow
me? I'm going to tell you something, once you get a little
grey hair on your head, and these kids today, and I don't
care who they are—black, yellow, or green—they'll grab
you for fifteen cents. . . . It's a way of life here. Who do
you know, what you can get out of it, who can support
your habit?

The host, a sophisticated urbanite, cannot imagine the pleasures
of rural life. "When you start to live in Vermont, I mean, after
you've gone down to the Exxon station and watched them grease
the car, what will you do next?" Evoking the image of earth, sky,
and nature, the sense of being united with one's surroundings, the

older gentleman reminds the audience that urban life does not exhaust the ways in which life can be happily lived.

> Well, listen, let me say it this way to you, there's plenty I can do. I can play darts, I can read, I can ski. I skied as a kid. I lived there for four years as a kid and my memories are still there. You can always remember what you did as a kid. Sure, I'll buy a horse. I'll buy a couple of cows. I can enjoy my life. I can't enjoy my life here. How can I enjoy my life here? It's unbelievable! I mean they hit your pocketbook—there's a new tax for everything. Everyday there's a new tax. All those politicians—Republicans and Democrats. . . . Where's the limit? When's it going to end?

Political corruption is a way of life—Democrats and Republicans. Party makes no difference, and the corruption continues—ever higher taxes are the price for cronyism and corruption. But this is not the most telling message. For this caller, one must escape to rural America to find peace: an open door at night, sleep without fear of intrusion, a peaceful old age in a rustic setting. The distance this man must traverse to find a life he considers more human is symbolic of how inhuman his present life appears to be.

The host, however, believes that rural life is an incredible bore. He and millions of Americans think of urban life as a positive trade-off. For excitement, sensate pleasure, culture, good food, fashion, sport, and so on, one accepts risks to life and property, filth, pollution, noise, bad transportation, "alien" races, intense competition, and fear. The trade-off has obviously been worth it for the more affluent.

Many American cities, however, are in serious trouble. People who care about their children, and who can afford to, move to the suburbs: the only place that their sons and daughters may possibly learn to read and write correctly. A new trade-off has occurred. The beat of the city, its amenities and culture, are foresaken for a suburban dream. The middle class opts for decent schools, the Parent-Teachers Association, a backyard with some grass, a hibachi, a basketball hoop, clean streets, Girl Scout cookies, and a shopping center with Bloomingdales. The civic complaints of most urban people will not be answered by the simple rustic life that the caller seeks.

This great move from the city to suburb has much to do with the alienation and anger that is the crisis of confidence. The caller plans to move to Vermont because his political birthright has been denied him and his safety has been threatened. He mistrusts, indeed loathes, city life. The American city has failed to create an agora, a public square where citizens may mature and govern through public discourse on the general will. The malaise of the city and flight from it are, in large part, the result of this political alienation, this sense that urban politics is not merely beyond public control but manipulated by self-interested elites. The excitement that once characterized big city elections has been replaced by the angry feeling that election day is a cruel hoax, a manipulation to determine which political cadre will plunder the city.

The caller is moving to Vermont for many reasons. His ultimate civic complaint, however, is that the city and the Commonwealth have failed to generate the critical political requisite: a common bond, a brotherhood, a general will, a public good, a common life. He may not know the philosophical underpinning that prompts his departure, but it lies in the belief that the public perspective of the Commonwealth has been fractured by the ferocity of private wills. Politics has become a separate culture—devious, private, and self-interested—and privatism has decimated the common cause. This senior citizen moves to Vermont to find what he lost in Massachusetts— res publica, real neighbors, and a little communal feeling.

Towards the end of the program a woman phones who was listening to the show while driving. She informs the host that she identifies so strongly with those who wish to leave Massachusetts that she parked and called from a pay phone.

> I would like to leave. I'll tell you why. I moved to Boston from New York City and I knew of Boston what every New Yorker knows, which is Beacon Hill, Harvard University, and a lot of interesting spots which are rather superficial that really don't tell you what the city truly is. Married my husband, who is from West Roxbury, moved to what's considered the best section in West Roxbury and last week two blocks from my house, a family had all of their walls painted and practically their house torn down because a black family came by to buy some furniture. And it sud-

denly hit me—wow—two blocks from my house—racism and this kind of terrible bigotry. And I never thought it would really hit me because I make a lot of money and so does my husband and we have a very nice home but it was right there looking me straight in the eye.

Well, there's no doubt that there exists a deep streak of racism in this town, but I might add that wherever you go, you'll see the same damn thing wherever you go.

Absolutely!

Miami, a town I know, it's another kind of racism. It's almost a paranoia when it comes to Spanish-speaking folks. You can't believe what people think about Spanish-speaking folks in Miami. It's paranoia.

I know what you mean. I'm Cuban. I know exactly what you mean. But you see . . . I . . . It's a totally different situation down there because you live within your community group and you fight back. And here I feel totally disenfranchised. And there is just no support whatsoever for someone like me to speak out.

The racism frightens and angers her, and since she is Latin, she is particularly concerned with what will happen to her children in a Boston public school.

I am also very concerned for example, about the school system because I would like my child to go to a public school, because I went to public schools and I do support the belief that that's really where you send your kid and support the community and integrate yourself to it, etc. But I see it as a terrible thing. I don't think the kid would get a good education and I really would feel that because I am Latin and the child's mother is Latin he would get a lot of terrible, negative reactions from that. So, I don't know. It's very depressing, and uh, it's a terrible let down for me.

The host suggests that she withdraw from public life.

Well, I guess what you have to do is you have to cut
yourself away from that. I mean you have to be almost
apolitical in a sense when it comes to that sort of thing.
I know it's hard for you to do that.

Yeah!

But after all the world is a large entity and in order to
stay you'll have to cut yourself away from that. That's all
there is to it.

The host suggests that she depoliticize herself, despite the fact
that she wishes to be a citizen in the classic sense, a full participant
in public life, a parent of a public school child, an active player in
community affairs—in other words, a model of Jeffersonian activism
and civic propriety. She seeks political fulfillment and power. He
counsels despair and withdrawal. Political alienation has been such
an old and deep-seated malaise in Massachusetts that he cannot envision a rebirth of popular power.
   This counsel of despair is difficult to accept.

Well, then how do you participate in the political process?
And how do you participate in the activities of the community where I do want to become a part of what's happening around me? And I have become a part in the past
of everything in other places that I lived: but here I'm just
not given a chance and it's very discouraging.

Here is a woman, obviously educated, caring, politically sophisticated, and successful, who cannot find roots in Boston; a woman
who wants to be part of the Commonwealth and yet feels that she
is denied some of the most elementary forms of political power. She
fears that she and her children will become victims of racism and
that she will be unable to do anything about it. She is a classic
alienated voter, for whom the crisis of confidence is immediate and
painful.
   She believes that she cannot utilize her profession, her skills, or
her political sentiment in the public service. She is truly alienated:
separated from the potential of a civic life and unable to control her
political surroundings. For her, American society has failed in sig-

nificant ways. Like millions of others who feel powerless, she is likely to withdraw from public life and make her life more private. Her children, home, husband, and work will become the focus of her life. She and millions of others support Rousseau's prediction that the modern world of self-interest will be a world in which egoism will triumph over public spirit.

For Rousseau and other critics of modernity, the world of individualism, with its egoistic imperatives, necessarily dissolves communal bonds. For such critics atomism threatened the life-enhancing community spirit provided by the university, church, guild, family, and the public project. The grand crisis of confidence for Rousseau, Hegel, Marx, and many other giants of social theory was rooted in the destruction of the general will and the common life. The disaster of the modern world is the displacement of the citizen–the man who seeks universal and public good—by the bourgeois seeker of self-interest, the practitioner of particularity.

But this is also the more permanent meaning of the crisis of confidence of the 1960s and 1970s. America is the manifestation of the modernist predicament. It is a welter of particularities, a web of competing private self-interests, in which the public constituency has been enfeebled. The liberal tradition of John Locke and Founding Fathers, with its emphases on private existence, private right, and private property, has not merely legitimized capitalism but also denigrated the concept of community.

The elevation of the private as the good and the denigration of the public as a tertiary virtue, has negated the value of a public life, the commonwealth that ultimately nourishes all and to which all are beholden. The bonds of sorority and fraternity, which nourish human growth and a sense of common interest, have been debilitated. The value placed on private right is now so great that the common good—a will transcending the sum of particularities—is difficult to imagine. Those who experience the crisis of confidence conceive it as the product of unmitigated self-interest, of the egoism that motivates the corrupt public servant and the marauding corporate executive. The inchoate but urgent wish for community is a symptom of what this crisis is ultimately about. The crisis of confidence in America is exemplified by the fact that America has no politics or discourse on the public good. There is ballyhoo, theatrics, symbolic manipulation, but no agora—no public center for disputation on the virtues of a common life. The historian and the disenfranchised Cuban woman testify to this.

The emotional and intellectual nourishment that might accrue to those who participate in public life is lost. We have no agora, no active public of any size, little urge to conceive of the common, and practically no personal growth through political participation. There is, in fact, no politics as the Greeks understood it.

This Cuban woman is one of alienated millions. She wants a public life. She seeks control of her life through public discourse, but is denied the participation and the power that it might bring. She is prevented from fulfilling the social aspect of her being that requires a public existence. The denial of a public life is her sorrow. Her civic complaint is compelling: powerlessness. She epitomizes those who experience a crisis of confidence.

5

I Looked in His Eyes and I Knew He Was a Crook

THE Commonwealth of Massachusetts is distinguished by its great universities and colleges, the achievements of high technology, and a long and notorious history of political corruption. Science, literature, and theft—the sacred and the profane are its legacy. The intellectually shrewd achievements of Digital, Wang, Polaroid, and Teradyne have been matched by the pragmatic and innovative designs of James Michael Curley and other mayors, and a small army of sheriffs, commissioners, state legislators, building inspectors. Indictments, convictions, suicides, resignations, denials, charges, countercharges, grand jury investigations, exposures, quid pro quo, nepotism, and delinquency are the dialectic of Massachusetts political life—so commonplace that large numbers of citizens have become alienated voters who feel powerless and plundered by politicians whom they believe are crooks and liars.

The democratic state is supposed to be a vehicle of popular sovereignty, a trustee of public right; but the alienated perceives it as oligarchy, a self-contained bureaucracy, an engine of self-aggrandizement. The alienated voter feels separated from his political birthright and stripped of his rightful political role by a state that has abandoned moral and legal restraint and abrogated its fiduciary obligation in the service of accumulating capital and power. The political world has been inverted. This inversion, this reversal of trust, law, and morality, creates the sense of separation that is alienation.

Politics in Washington, however, is no less venal than politics in Boston, according to one caller whose despair is typical.

You think it's different in Washington? Maybe in some ways, maybe fewer crooks, but Watergate makes you wonder. The Washington corruption is different and more arrogant. In the middle of inflation with 10 million unemployed they raise their salaries. Nobody controls them. Posh junkets all around the world—supposed to get information—basically government paid vacations—the VIP treatment all the way—and it doesn't cost a penny. Dozens of congressmen hardly even attend, but they do appoint their wives and daughters to their office staff. That's good for another forty. But the Washington guys are just like Massachusetts, they are invited to speak at universities about the future of America and go to fancy parties—but most of them are on the make—in Washington and Boston—stakes may be different, the way they do it may be different, but it all stinks.

The alienated voter knows why men and women enter political life. It is certainly not to serve the public or to promote a particular ideology. The motivation is more pragmatic and self-serving.

Why would anyone enter politics? Why would they make a career of it—stay in the House for thirty years? The pay is not that great. You could make much more in business. Why would anyone put up with all that crap—endless meetings, boring, stupid people, favors, thousands of letters to answer—being away from home—people around your neck all the time? You know what the answer is? There are secret benefits, under the table benefits. I'm talking about selling favors and contracts and jobs. Don't worry, there's money in politics—plenty of money if you want it and all kinds of ways of hiding it. Who gets caught? Practically no one. You got to be stupid to get caught. This is why most people go into politics and stay there. Big money, my boy. And the higher up you are the better your opportunities. More power, more graft.

"You know how you make money in politics?" one caller remarked. "Not by enforcing the law, but by selective enforcement of the law."

This comment provoked the liberal host to reaffirm the first principle of Massachusetts politics: quid pro quo. "They play their little game, their little game of lobbying, with this guy and what have you done for me. I'll do this for you if you do this for me. That the game of Massachusetts politics, and it's the same way at City Hall." A caller quickly responds, "It's exactly the same thing . . . they're blood-suckers and parasites on you and me. We work."

The prelude to power, the political campaign, is an exercise in duplicity, a billingsgate of innuendo, a masquerade of false promises and lies designed to entice the uninitiated and comfort the alienated. The alienated voter, confronted with candidates who lie and slander, candidates who specialize in the false promises and the illusion, assumes that campaigns and the outcomes of elections are meaningless.

This lament was provoked by November elections:

> **What's the point in voting? In the first place, all you get from the candidates is a lot of bull, a lot of phony promises that they use during elections but never fulfill. If all the promises become real, Massachusetts would be a utopia. It's all a pack of lies. But there is another reason for not voting, another reason why elections are phony. The power is all locked up. You get a monopoly of power in the legislature, a monopoly of power in City Hall. The mayor and the heads of the legislature control everything—the favors, the jobs, the contracts. Everybody owes them and they owe nobody. So when an election does take place, what difference does it make? Whoever gets elected they go to kowtow to the boss.**

Political power is monopolized and abused, and popular sovereignty is an illusion. Instead, oligarchy and collusion are the reality. Political culture and popular culture are disjoined. The issue is power and the abuse of power. If politicians are venal, masters of quid pro quo, what can the state be but a perversion? For the alienated voter, the state has become precisely what Marx predicted it would be: an executive committee of the ruling class, an alliance for the mutual enrichment of statesmen and businessmen. The state is a mutual aid society, from which the public is excluded. The politician needs campaign contributions, kick-backs and bribes, while the contractor, the tavern owner, the insurance company, the real estate operator, the plumber, the electrician, the architect, the podiatrist, and the restauranteur need contracts, preferential treatment, licenses, tax abatements, or permits. The state has become an agency for the production and reproduction of capital for itself and its clients; it is a tax-free business where profit bears little relation to public service.

> Politics is cash and carry, no credit, no promises. It's all in who you know, a matter of credentials. To get a contract for a building it's one or two state reps and a city counselor. A different guy for a tax abatement and another one for highway construction. I know, I'm in the construction business—for thirty years. You don't believe in bidding, the largest bidder! Bids have practically nothing to do with getting most jobs. Who you know, that's it. I think more or less everything's for sale or for a favor. You got to know the ropes. The city is worse. Sometimes many guys are involved—split the pie. And you know they take care of each other, particularly when it's time to retire. There are plenty of seats on state boards and commissions for all of them. It's like a big family. Nobody forgets their brothers and friends. It has nothing to do with elections, nothing to do with public service. These guys have their own rules. They go their own way and they are married to each other. Republicans too.

Political alienation is a response to the perception of the state as a separate and self-serving culture. The alienated voter is without influence, an outsider who is no longer part of the political process. The contractor is alienated because the state has violated its fiduciary obligation to his profession by substituting nepotism for merit quid pro quo for equity. And he has been hurt in the process: his sense of political efficacy is low. The state for him is an autonomous force, an immobile and unresponsive leviathan that is immune to public pressure. He structures the political world dichotomously into insiders who are powerful and voters who are powerless. He does not believe that elections significantly affect the political process or enhance his self-interest. His anger is compounded by the fact that he thinks he knows who the villains are, but can do nothing about it.

The conspiracy of silence and cash that is the state remains ultimately elusive, a recognized yet hidden enemy.

How can you tell one from another? Aren't they all the same? You don't see them accept bribes or exchange favors, or make appointments. But you know for years that they do it. The other caller was right. It's who you know and how much cash you have. He's right, everything for sale, no receipts, no books. So why not believe all do it. The profits are big. The risks are small. When is the last time somebody got caught? You tell me. There is another rule you can follow: why do guys give big money to candidates? Let's not kid ourselves. They want something in return and they get it. The size of the contribution is the price; bigger prize, bigger price. And since only big guys can offer this, they get the big contracts and get richer.

It's poor slobs like us that work for wages. We have no clout. It's only insiders and Mr. Biggie, who can understand the temptation? Not many? So it all adds up. They're all in it, they're all big men. The higher up the political ladder, the worse. It's sad isn't it? And who's gonna clean it up? (laughter) Nobody ever has.

The disenchanted are wary of all things political: candidates who spend large amounts of money, candidates endorsed by the powerful and celebrated. Bigness—big money, big indebtedness, big power, big operators, big campaigners—are all suspect. It is not surprising that the alienated voter, denied his sovereign power, suspects the great American virtues of bigness and power. The web of suspicion is without limit. Political alienation becomes a self-fulfilling prophecy. Good men are corrupted by the rules of the political game.

Political alienation may also be experienced as meaninglessness, as the belief that candidates do not provide adequate information for rational political choices. The alienated electorate perceives candidates as liars and cheats. The words of politicians are not believable; campaign promises are false and invective is self-serving. The campaign is a meaningless enterprise because the trust necessary for a confident decision is absent and the information necessary for a rational choice is insufficient. Candidates are supposed to offer meaningful alternatives and information that gives citizens confidence in their integrity and intentions. Political alienation, in the form of meaninglessness, may be experienced in two quite different ways. A citizen may feel an election is without significance because no real differences exist among the candidates, or he may feel that rational decision is impossible because the meaningful information he needs is lacking. If the candidates and platforms are very similar or identical, or if the voter refuses to give credence to campaign promises or invective, it is impossible to make a rational choice.

> **As I walk to the voting booth, all I remember is one guy pointing his finger, some woman walking through the woods staring into space, and some guy who keeps claiming he is different from everybody else. There's five of 'em, just the three I remember, pointing his finger, the woman walking through the woods. . . . Everyone's like that, I'm going in blind. Eenie, meenie, minie, moe.**

The host senses the humor of the call and opts for more. The caller asks, "Who is the Republican candidate for lieutenant governor?" "Easy enough, sir." "Here is a multiple choice contest. You ready? What is a Leon Lombardi? a) an Italian sports car, b) a restaurant in the North End, c) a state representative, or d) a candidate for lieutenant governor?"

The exchange is instructive because it contains a double mockery of the meaninglessness experienced by this alienated caller. The caller remembers neither the names nor the faces of the candidates. All are identified by absurd and politically irrelevant actions depicted in political advertisements—pointing, walking, staring. The candidates, already faceless and without identity, are transformed into disembodied and reified models. The caller further dehumanizes politicians when the possibility is raised that Leon Lombardi, a candidate, may be a sports car or a restaurant. "Eenie, meenie, minie, moe," he responds. Williams has the final word. "The election is Tuesday. About thirty percent of the people will show up. The rest of them will be eating Chinese food."

> **Hi, my name is Robert Meany Cappucci, your Democratic candidate for United States Congress in the Eighth**

Congressional District. Robert Meany Cappucci has campaigned for your vote. Robert Meany Cappucci needs your
vote. Remember to vote Robert Meany Cappucci, September 14th, Primary Day. Have a nice day. Paid for by the
Committee to Elect Bob Cappucci to Congress, Eighth
Congressional District. Thank you.

Mr. Cappucci's announcement is meaningless, without content,
but not without a latent message for the alienated. "Have a nice day"
is not a typical politician's greeting. It is too relaxed, too informal,
and too unceremonial for a professional politician. Perhaps Mr. Cappucci expected to differentiate himself from the typical Massachusetts politician. Nevertheless, the advertisement replicates the
campaign: it is vacuous. The caller seeks more information. "Who
is Robert Meany Cappucci" the host can not permit Cappucci's sim-
ple-mindlessness to go unnoticed. He imitates the voice of Dracula:

Ladies and gentlemen, who is Robert Meany Cappucci?

I don't know. I see his name on the backs of buses and
he looks tough.

Everybody looks tough this year. This is the year of tough-
ness. I'm the only one who's soft. I'm soft on smut.

But no one is talking about the issues.

Robert Meany Cappucci designs jeans. (laughter) Have a
cup of Cappucci.

Williams turns the campaign into a shambles. He not only performs with a Dracula-like voice, suggesting that Cappucci is one of
a chamber of political horrors, but he reifies and humiliates Cappucci:
a cup of Cappucci. In more prosaic and less symbolic terms, the
caller is saying exactly the same thing, "No one is saying anything
and it's frustrating." This is political alienation in the form of
meaninglessness.

Alienated callers object to the negativism of the campaigns, and
to the counterpoint of attack and counterattack. They want but
cannot find meaningful discussions of the issues. They want to cast
a rational vote, but cannot.

All those negative, negative commercials—it's been really difficult watching all these people getting busted in the chops. . . . rather than saying vote for me because I'm the good guy and I know what's going on and I'll take care of you, they're saying don't vote for him. He's the bad guy and hasn't done anything right. I'd like to take the 5 million spent on the campaign and use it a lot better than calling issues that are not really issues. And the people sort of miss this year the real issues.

The alienated concur: the campaign is a circus, a madcap burlesque in which comedy and cruelty fuse in a spectacle that is both absurd and fascinating.

This is the first time I have voted in Massachusetts in the governor's race and it is quite a circus. I've never experienced this before and I think that the millions that was spent by the two candidates attacking each other is fascinating. . . . Dukakis went after King and King went after Dukakis and it got to be quite ugly with the tape nonsense and all the other garbage.

The conservative host, who is customarily predisposed to view the electoral process as a meaningful channel of public choice, concurred.

I happened to hear on the news that both campaigns were saying how they focused on the issues and didn't let this campaign become a matter of personalities. Good heavens! This has been one of the lowest, one of the most vicious, hateful campaigns that I can remember, and they're all proud that they focused on the issue. The issue being, we hate our opponent.

The vicious interchange, the unremitting barrage of invective, may be meaningless, but it may also give pleasure to the alienated voter because it confirms his suspicions. The candidates prove the suspicion that politicians are venal and cheap and that campaigns are without meaning. The campaign confirms the self-fulfilling prophecy and becomes another documentation of political debasement.

The alienated may take pleasure in the low blow and the bitter exchange, but they are frustrated because these tactics foreclose discussion of the issues. They are alienated precisely because they seek meaning.

> He's got the white hat on. Dukakis does not want to face the issues. He was the worst governor we ever had. . . . He had a corrupt government. . . . I just can't stand by and hear this fellow tell how clean he is with the white hat. . . . This poor Eddy King has got to go through lie detector tests and his family got to be dragged through the mud. It's really not fair. Politics was not meant for that. What about the issues?

> You try to find out who's for what. All you hear is the other guy's a bum. And when they start talking with all that high tone stuff about budgets and surpluses and cities and towns, you either can't understand it or you know it's a lot of bull which is supposed to impress you. It's hard to tell who's a Democrat and who isn't. In the old days you knew Saltonstall was a Republican and Kennedy was a Democrat. You knew that Democrats were for working men and Republicans were for the rich. Now you don't even know who is in what party and, if you did, it wouldn't do you much good. You know they all hate each other, but that doesn't help you much to vote. It's all in the gutter. How do you know who to hate?

The campaign is a *Three Penny Opera* sung by fools and scoundrels. Political talk radio delegitimizes political campaigns through ridicule and accurate reportage. Callers believe American politics is obscene, and both conservative and liberal hosts—for quite different reasons—sense the surrealistic and gross nature of the political life that they satirize with artistry. Their prototypes are the buffoon, the pompous ass, the preprogrammed marionette, the scoundrel, and the party dunce. They subject the public, as well as the politician, to ridicule. Williams' capacity for satire was exhibited when thou-

sands of outraged citizens joined in a nightly crusade to ban a por-
nographic bookstore. They picketed, chanted "The Battle Hymn of
the Republic," prayed, and preached in a replay of Ibsen's *Enemy of
the People*. The host consistently defended the bookstore's right to
operate. The townspeople formed a committee, Save Our Stough-
ton—SOS; Williams advocated the formation of a new civil liberties
group, Save Our Smut.

> Saving our smut . . . there's a new gang called the smut
> majority. The pro-smut majority gathering strength.
> There's going to be a large rally for people who are in
> favor of smut. It's called the silent smut majority.

The death penalty also evokes Williams' ire. His remarks illustrate
the capacity of talk radio to delegitimize. A female caller announces
that she will vote for Governor King.

> Yes, only because I heard Governor Dukakis say that he is
> going to veto the death penalty. . . . Everybody's getting
> murdered off and raped and nobody's paying for any-
> thing, for any of their bad things. It's just not right.
>
> They're all on the street, right?
>
> Right.
>
> I thought they were all in the Charles Street Jail . . . all
> in jail. And you're all for capital punishment. That's a good
> woman for you . . . kind, generous, and loyal.
>
> I think a murderer should have their just dues.
>
> Do you know what I'm for doing? I'm for frying them at
> ten o'clock at night on television. I'm for electrocuting
> them, so all of it can come up on TV. . . . I want to see
> the governor come out and introduce him and say, "We'll
> be back in a moment with the electrocution, but first, let
> me do a couple of commercials. . . . Public hangings in
> the Common. You bet, I'm in favor of that.

The alienated voter knows the surrealistic and inverted character
of politics, and this is precisely why it is so difficult to make rational

choices. Every political actor wears a mask. Public officials are sellers of favors; campaign contributors are buyers. Politics is cash and carry, a financial market specializing in options. The state is a cash nexus of politicians and brokers where everything is reduced to profit and loss. Nothing is what it appears to be. The issue for the alienated voter is not merely to seek the lesser evil, but to differentiate between symbolic embodiments of evil. Political talk radio is unique among the mass media because it captures this surrealism, and, through the use of parody, suggests that what appears to be real is, in fact, absurd.

The alienated voter must make some sense of this inverted reality: he wishes to cut his losses. Elections in which the alienated play a significant role are not won by any candidate because there is no affirmation. The alienated voter does not vote for anyone, but against the greater evil. Candidates win by default. They win because their opponent is perceived as more venal, more banal, or more political. Incumbents, therefore, are disadvantaged. They have a political history; they are politicians. Their innocence is demonstrably lost.

It is not easy for the alienated to discern gradations of evil. The customary criteria for voting—class, ideology, ethnicity, race, party affiliation—are suspended. Words have lost their meaning and promises are empty. Party affiliation is negated by bilateral corruption. Ideology is rubbish. Defamation is counterproductive. One Bostonian epitomized the situation years ago: "It takes a crook to know one."

The alienated voter attends to the style of candidates: their visage and posture become signs of their being. The shape of a mouth, the cut of a suit, the twinkle of an eye, the fullness or paucity of hair, or the timbre of voice become signs of lesser or greater dishonesty. "I looked in his eyes and I knew he was a crook." "He's a smug bastard with his cigars." "I don't like his voice, there's something about his eyes." "He just looks crooked." These are responses of Boston voters sampled at random in the 1960s. "He's too polished, the biggest stuffed shirt I have ever seen." "Look at his clothes. He's definitely a lady's man." Callers in the 1980s reiterate the theme, "All you have to do is look at that son of a bitch and you know he'll take every nickel we have." "I wouldn't trust anybody with eyes like that." "Look at that face. It's flat, no nose, not for me." "I don't like to knock anyone, but you know that slogan from the Bible about how it's harder for a camel to get through the eye of a needle than it is for an honest man to enter the kingdom of heaven. Well, I have said enough. Look at 'em. You think they're goin' to make it to the kingdom of heaven?"

The nose, the eyes, the cut of the suit, the subtle gesture may also be taken as a positive sign. "He spoke to you with his heart, not his head." "Just the way he spoke, I feel he's honest." "He had a nice quiet manner." "Anybody who dresses so nice must be nice." These are gut reactions, intuitive and visceral responses, intimate, personal, idiosyncratic, and completely unpredictable. A nice quiet manner may be an assset to one alienated voter, to another it may be a sign of stupidity or impotence. The permutations are endless. Even the most experienced political strategists will be tested by these responses.

To some, clothes make the man. On election day, 1982, Jerry Williams and his callers discuss their reaction to how candidates present themselves—dress and grooming. "Dukakis hasn't changed that much," reports one observer of dress, "this is the same guy you know."

> Well, it is easy to do. Do you want off-the-rack Sears Roebuck? Or do you want polyester?
>
> No! No! King's got a couple of good suits.
>
> I didn't notice them.
>
> No! No! He has got a couple of good suits.
>
> Well, then, he's got to change his shirts.
>
> No; his shirts are pretty nice, too.
>
> A little worn around the edges.
>
> They got wrinkled in the helicopter, but you see him in the morning before the . . .
>
> You take a look at the paper yesterday and you see a picture of Dukakis wearing button-down stripes and King with a bad knot in his tie.
>
> But they wore the same suit in the debate.
>
> Everybody wore the same suit.

An acerbic woman joins the discussion and suggests that since King and Dukakis are equally banal, the best way to decide is on the basis of which one is better looking. Williams protests but his guest insists. "I don't care, Jerry, Dukakis is cute and I voted for him because he's cute. Why not? What worries me is that his wife has that phony, sickening smile."

The physical presence of the candidate, registered in infinite and idiosyncratic ways, is critical for the alienated. The presentation of self in everyday life, filtered through gut reaction, is what matters, not the presentation of issues. The format of the campaign is determined by the standard political protocols: a campaign is supposed to be serious, dignified, meaningful, and ideological. Candidates are supposed to discuss something called issues. But most veteran campaigners know that issues are, for the most part, relics of a more simple age, aspects of the archaic rules of a game to which lip service must be paid. The intimacy of television has hastened the demise of these rules by highlighting the lip, eye, hair, smile, and sweat.

Hundreds of callers testify to the irrelevance of issues and the relevance of personae. A case in point is the response of a woman to John Sears, a Republican candidate for governor of Massachusetts in 1982—a most proper Bostonian, a long-time public servant, and a former Rhodes Scholar.

Hi Jerry. Oh Jerry. I know that you had John Sears the other day and I know that every time I look at him on the tube, for some reason or other, my thoughts go to what he looks like. If you talk to him again, he has too much face.

Too much face, meaning his suits are too dark?

No, darling, a horse face. He should let his hair grow long, more casual, and he'd be more attractive.

In other words, his face, because of the close haircut makes him look all face. You might be right.

How do campaign managers determine the vote-maximizing hairdo when some prefer a bouffant style and others are attracted to a crewcut? The importance of hair and cut interests callers.

Your last caller was right. After all Harshbarger [a candidate for district attorney used to have a Haldeman type crewcut and he softenened his hair style and won.

Haldeman, when you have that crewcut you look like a Nazi. Right?

Right.

He let his hair grow after he got out of the White House, let his hair grow a little softer so he had a soft look to him, and Harshbarger did the same thing, right?

Right, it probably took months off his sentence.

John Sears obviously does have close-cropped hair, which sort of does give a round appearance to his head. He wears dark clothes and a white shirt and, obviously, that all sort of reflects upward. Right?

You may be right.

"Dukakis comes across very well," reports a female caller. The host interjects, "What do you mean by 'comes across'?"

How he presents himself, how he dresses. . . . I didn't like Mrs. King's reaction when her husband lost, not very appropriate for a lady.

What did you want her to do—break down and cry?

No, I wanted her not to move. I'd like her to stay like a lady. . . . King, no matter where you look, you know he's hiding things. I want her to be more reserved. I don't want her to pretend she is someone else. Mike Dukakis' wife, there's another case. She stands there, never moves, looks like the real lady, always polite and soft spoken. I can't stand it, all that phony aristocracy. Who does she think she is? I bet she is not like that in real life.

The distinction between real life and political life is the issue. Pretense, artifact, and theatrics are the essence of political life; it is illusion. This is why intuition and disbelief are appropriate. This is why the mind of the alienated voter is arcane and unpredictable. This is why campaign strategy becomes counterphobic, hazardous, and increasingly randomized.

Sweat makes the man, particularly in an inverted world where candidates assume the mantle of Buster Keaton and John Wayne. Jerry Williams comments on Edward King's television performance.

I guess one of the big factors is that Ed King simply is not a TV performer. Every time he gets out before the cameras in any sort of a situation that is not completely and utterly preplanned, even if it is planned or replanned, everybody is nervous. He's tense, he's sweating, I'm sweating, while he's sweating, watching him. I'm nervous for him and nobody knew how to handle Ed King. Ed King just came off as tense, nervous, sweating all the time. And Dukakis always comes along as relaxed and easy-going and looking like someone who is at ease. While the other guy, King, always looks like he is very upset with nobody taking a picture of him at any time. Is that a fair thing to say or no?

To one voter sweat can signify nervousness and guilt, to another it may be a sign of honest labor.

The governor is jumpy. He is a nervous guy—worried looking. He's got something on his mind. I think he hides things. He's got somethin' to hide.

Dukakis won because he did two things—remained quiet and cool and talked seriously about the issues. He stayed above the fray, cool statesman, nonpolitician, little attacking of his opponent. He's a candidate who talks seriously. He is not a hood. He is boring, and he is cold, but he doesn't look like a politician.

After two days of postelection talk, a woman phones the Jerry Williams show.

I used to be very involved in politics and I used to debate then and yell and scream at people, all that junk, so now

I vote for people who are cute. It's the only way to do it. I know you are going to yell at me for that.

Michael's cute?

Yeah, very. Cute, that's the word. Sexy, sexy.

How tall are you?

Five-three, just about your size.

How about Sears?

Boring.

Both of them are now planning on how to manipulate, how to get rid of these perceptions, one is boring, a nice man, a fatherly figure. Michael is now trying to give that image of being cool, detached. What should they talk about? What is the most important thing you are concerned about?

Survival, survival of the economy.

The economy may interest some voters, but the overriding issue is political corruption and credibility. The pervasiveness of corruption exacerbates the crisis of confidence. Mistrust negates the relevance of traditional voting criteria. The intuitive reaction replaces the calculation of economic self-interest.

King, when you look at him, you know he's hiding something, no matter where he is. They are all crooks, every one of them. It doesn't make any difference what party. Massachusetts politics has been corrupt for so long that stealing is okay. It's the normal thing to do. And almost everybody does it and gets away with it, Democrats and Republicans. So many politicians have been doing it for so long that no politician thinks there's anything wrong with it. There is not stigma to it. This is the Massachusetts way. And despite the fact that we have so many indictments and convictions—look at King's administration— the majority get away with it. It's not only that they steal, that they give their cousins and aunts and friends jobs—

high-paying jobs, jobs for life. The government is like one big family. So, somebody yells, but nothing happens. This is a way of life.

This is the complaint of the alienated voter: crime, but no punishment. No candidate escapes suspicion. One day after Michael Dukakis was elected to his second term as governor of Massachusetts, largely on the basis of his reputation as an honest and nonpolitical man, a contractor phones Jerry Williams.

I believe that Duke has sold his soul, sold his soul to all the contractors who put the money up there for him in the beginning of his primary. He owes more than King ever owed in the form of favors. We're not going to get any contracts in the future administration unless we contribute. So I think that stuff has already started.

Williams asks the contractor to phone after the show and tell him. "You've got yourself a big story."

Well, this is a problem. We can't afford to do that. If we do that we're going to be out completely. We've been looking at selling out the business and moving to another state. . . . We've been dealing with attorney general on some of these pressures. But the trouble with the attorney general's office is that you've got a Democrat in there and they don't want to know too much now. . . . It's not that I want to vote for the Republicans, it's a question of voting against what I know is going on.

The critical issue is not the reality of corruption, but the web of suspicion. Widespread corruption is taken, correctly or incorrectly, as a matter of fact—the a priori of Massachusetts political life. Politicians are guilty until proven innocent; the billingsgate of invective and rumor is unbounded. There is no solid ground, which is why illusion fuses with reality. This is why campaigning and voting become idiosyncratic and irrational.

Conservatives are saddened by this mistrust and irrationality. Avi Nelson comments on this situation.

I think I agree with you that the corruption issue ultimately was the one that spelled the margin of difference.
But let me ask this. What is it about us—and I use the
word "us" here as the electorate—what is it about us that
we would take the word of an advanced liar and thief
and elevate the man to a position of prominence in the
campaign? How could we do that?

A caller provides the popular, common-sense answer.

Because we are all focused in on corruption in politics.
We all believe that politicians are crooks, we all have a
distrust of all politicians and it is simply a terrible thing
that we are facing in the future.

The origins of the crisis of confidence transcend particular corrupt
acts of politicians. They lie in the belief that a new political culture
has emerged, a culture of amorality and illegality, a culture of quid
pro quo and nepotism, a political culture antithetical to the public
interest. The state has separated itself from the public purpose, and
millions of citizens have separated themselves from the political
process.

Jerry Williams describes the political culture of the Bay State, a
culture of dynastic ambition and feudal obligation, a culture remi-
niscent of the Italian city-states during the time of the Medici.

These guys are not members of the Democratic Party. They
are not liberals, they are not in the liberal tradition of
great Massachusetts Democrats—John McCormack, John
Kennedy, Tip O'Neill. They belong to the party of George
Wallace. . . . They want to expand the private sector.
They want to diminish public services—welfare and aid
to the poor—and they want as much of government business turned over to the private sector as possible.

But what they really are is the party of cronyism, the party
of the buddy system. You take care of me and I'll take
care of you. Everybody's cousin and aunt gets a state job.
Everybody takes care of his buddies. Bill Bulger [president

of the Massachusetts State House] has five relatives on the payroll, five relatives, can you imagine that? And he doesn't see a thing wrong with it. None of them see anything wrong with it. They all do it. And King appoints the brothers and sisters, sons and daughters of state representatives and senators and city counselors.

This is incest. It's blatant and they see nothing wrong with it. This is our culture—a new culture. This is our political culture. The incestuous culture. It's worse than the old Curley days. Much worse. This is incest, whether you like the word or not. And it's the norm. It's okay. It's not wrong anymore. It's a new set of rules. And what about the people? The hell with them.

On occasion, and with much amusement, callers relate personal experiences that indicate their familiarity with the culture of corruption and cronyism. A militant King supporter tells Williams that he would vote for the governor, "because he's getting the chiselers off welfare."

He's what?

Getting the fakers off welfare. I have four in my family, I know.

You have four fakers in your family?

One was a plumber making over twelve dollars an hour and he owns his own home. Another one had $23,000 in the bank and was collecting subsidized rent. Another one who made $6,000 on a home she sold is on social security and had her rent subsidized. Another brother is a roofer.

Let's get these fakers off welfare. . . . He wants to get them off welfare and the only way he knows how is to vote for King. He can't throw them out of the house.

The inversion of public and private life evokes an inversion of public and private expectation. Campaign strategy becomes surrealistic and theatrical. Alienated voters seek the face behind the mask.

Politics becomes pathology. Candidates, for example, may know that voters discount their words, but they do not know what to say; they may know content gives way to form, but they have little or no idea of what pleases the eye. The result is madcap campaigns that unintentionally parody Buster Keaton and the Marx brothers. Lunacy, fabrication, artifice and nonsense transform politics into a grotesque masquerade—a degradation of the democratic process. Candidates and strategists, bewildered by the alienated constituency, use common sense as their guide; however, it is frequently counterproductive.

Operating on the assumption that the character of candidates, not issues, is critical, they defame the opposition. Slander is the order of the day. Since purity may be a virtue, candidates present themselves as forever virginal. Political virginity may be a great asset in a universe of corrupt politicians, and politicians strive in most amusing ways to deny their profession. The Calvin Coolidge gambit is favored by Protestants—a fusion of aloofness, class, sobriety, silence, and crusty New England aphorisms. Reticence and class, it is assumed, convey an aversion to power; piety conveys rectitude.

In a world of crooks and liars, it is easy to assume that the best strategy is to stereotype the opposition as crooks, masters of deceit, vendors of the public interest, and specialists in laundered campaign contributions. Strategists, in other words, project the ugly stereotypes held by the alienated onto the opposition. The campaign becomes a torrent of invective and counterinvective, a parade of puppets led by a good soldier and and a good fairy. The issue is portrayed as David and Goliath.

The campaign becomes lunatic because the alienated electorate forces campaigners to become irrational. The strategist intuits the importance of gut reactions and then pursues symbolic gambits that he believes will tap the mysteries of the ids and superegos of alienated voters.

The candidate, for example, often addresses issues in a highly sophisticated and detailed way, not because his speech writer believes the content of the speech affects voters positively, but because its academic tone will be taken as a sign that the candidate is knowledgeable and caring—and therefore not political. This is a typical Kennedy stratagem. The medium becomes the message, and form triumphs over content. Doublespeak and latent symbolism replace straight talk.

The significance of the medium as the message became clear when the liberal host interviewed a fellow from Harvard's Kennedy School of Government concerning the gubernatorial contest between Michael Dukakis and Edward King.

> King's ads have been emotional ads, symbolic ads, whereas Dukakis's ads have tried to convey a rational linear message, not exciting to people.

> The Democrats originally wanted him to charge up the mountain—bugles blowing, retake the high ground, they expected to be led on a wild and romantic mission. Instead they have been led to toil in lowlands, working on the unromantic minutiae of the campaign organization.

The man from the Kennedy School perceives that the proper object of the campaign should not be to inform and educate, not an exercise in reason or logic; it should be an effort to generate votes through high emotion.

> King provides much more symbolic leadership. He's ready to talk about the big picture. He's ready to make a leap from mandatory sentencing to drug pushers, to fighting drugs. Whereas Dukakis is a lawyer. He thinks rationally, literally, and he says, "Gee, I'm not sure there's a connection there. So I can't tell people there's a connection there." He made a lawyer's brief for why it was okay to ban the bookstore that sells smut. That's all well and good, it has nothing to do with politics. Nothing to do with inspiring people, nothing to do with generating an emotional committment to his candidacy.

Despite this standard wisdom, emotive rhetoric may be counterproductive for an alienated electorate because it is strident and aggressive—that is, typically political. It is the rhetoric of those who seek power. It may be more effective to do what Dukakis did: campaigning seriously on the issues, without rancor, without invective; quietly and continually exposing malfeasance and private license; reiterating the theme of public service and equity; enjoying the image of the amateur David—a bit naive, but thoroughly committed. The appropriate ego ideal may be Jimmy Stewart in *Mr. Smith Goes to Washington*.

The seemingly naive and dull Dukakis strategy—a lawyer's brief, the high ground—may be the best approach because the sober message, graphs, and facts and figures appear to be unpolitical and scholarly. Sobriety and scholarship may create an aura of otherworldliness.

"Symbolic leadership," high emotion, and "the big picture," may have great appeal, but not for the generally accepted reasons. Mandatory sentencing, the fight against drugs, opposition to abortion, and endorsement of school prayer may attract the alienated voter, but not because of their ideological content. Instead, it is because they are perceived as moral issues, matters of good and evil. Such issues transcend crass political considerations and appear to have little to do with politics. The moral posture of the candidate places him beyond politics and defines him as a preacher not a politician. He becomes the occupant of a higher ground. Ronald Reagan's election in 1984, usually interpreted in terms of economic issues, had much to do with moral posturing. The seemingly transcendant ethic of the moral majority makes the preacher of the politician.

The talk shows aired during the 1982 Massachusetts election reveal the Alice-in-Wonderland quality of an alienated political culture. John Kerry—now U.S. senator from Massachusetts, a founder of Vietnam Veterans against the War, an articulate civil rights activist, and a committed liberal of the Kennedy stripe—campaigned for lieutenant governor in 1982. His approach to the alienated voter, though comic and adolescent, may have been effective.

There is something fishy going on in our state government, (sound of water) bribery, pay-offs, kick-backs, envelopes stuffed with cash. It seems every time you watch the news, you find crooked politicians or bureaucrats have taken the bait. (sound of water slurping) What this state needs in high office is people with records of enforcing the law, not ignoring it. John Kerry is the only lieutenant gubernatorial candidate who has that record. As a criminal prosecutor, John Kerry put New England's number two crime boss behind bars, and as first assistant district

attorney, he started a White Collar Crime Unit and broke up a government bribery conspiracy. John Kerry knows (water slurping) how to fish for a catch, the corrupt politicians who takes a dive into the tank. (sound of diving into water) Massachusetts could sure use his help. John Kerry, first on the ballot for the second-highest office in this state. Lieutenant Governor John Kerry will make that office what it should be: second-strongest. Paid for by the Kerry Committee.

Kerry might have discussed the issues, or enunciated his progressive views, or explained what a lieutenant governor does. However, he opted with good reason to woo the disenchanted and summarized, in sixty seconds, the litany of the alienated voter: bribery, pay-offs, kick-backs, envelopes stuffed with cash, crooked politicians and bureaucrats, and the desire for honesty and law enforcement. He affirmed his status as a criminal prosecutor, allegedly a nonpolitical posture of rectitude. The bait-and-hook format is puerile perhaps, but the stereotypes are there: the elusive catch and the shrewd fisherman, hunter and hunted. The criminal prosecutor casts himself in the image of Tom Dewey and Clint Eastwood. The scenario of alienated voters is the scenario of the Western sheriffs and outlaws, good and evil.

Because strategists have little or no idea of what appeals to alienated voters, they opt for the bizarre and exotic, on the assumption that satire and surrealism will temper mistrust.

Lois Pines, a proper, suburban, middle class, liberal state representative and an opponent of Kerry, appealed to voters with the following advertisement.

Here's one more voice in the fight for lieutenant governor. I'm Mohammed Ali telling you to get out there and pull the lever for Lois Pines. (crowd noise) She's running for lieutenant governor. Lois Pines, lieutenant governor for Massachusetts. Vote for her or I'll bust your nose.

[Announcer:] Lois Pines for lieutenant governor (crowd noise) because we need a special leader to fight the special interests. Paid for by the Lois Pines Committee.

This adolescent lapse of taste illustrates how bewildered campaigners are. Assuming that the alienated voter wants a knockout punch delivered to corruption, but unaware of how the alienated voter selects the lesser evil, Pines opts for the ultimate puncher, Mohammed Ali, who busts noses of bad guys.

John Kerry and Lois Pines have recreated themselves and have produced an image for public consumption that bears little resemblance to their real selves. They do not talk or act this way in real life: John Kerry does not speak of catching corrupt fish, and Lois Pines does not bust people's noses. They have banalized, stupified, and reified themselves in an effort to create personae believable to the alienated voter. They have lost themselves in this transvaluation and have presented themselves as metaphors to their constituency. The campaign becomes a series of crafted illusions, a world of stick figures. The alienated voter, believing that politics is a deception, gives birth to candidates who deceive. One illusion compounds another. Everyone believes that nothing is what it appears to be.

The stereotypical images of the alienated voter, though possibly realistic, leads candidates to create counterstereotypes—the dominant image is that of Tom Dewey, the criminal prosecutor, the vengeful sheriff, the man of impeccable personal morals, the champion of law and order. The Richard Nixon stereotype is also common: the innocent but wrongfully accused do-gooder, surrounded by conspiratorial felons who libel and slander. The Edward Kennedy stick figure is also popular: the righteous progressive, the beautiful person, whose wealth and class free him of the need to be corrupt. The candidate presents himself as a nonpolitician who takes the high road by presenting issues in terms of "apolitical" statistics, not cheap invective. The Reagan-like puppet, the patriot-moralist basking in the righteousness of school prayer and the right to life, is also a popular nonpolitical favorite. Art replicates life.

Normal voting criteria have been suspended; traditional campaign strategies have been suspended. The suspension is a response to mistrust. The alienated voter responds to arcane psychological and intuitive cues. The issue is vengeance, disgust, anger, cynicism, powerlessness, and frustration. The campaign becomes an arena for projection, a psychodrama, a pseudomorality play. Psychological catharsis becomes significant. The campaign becomes stage and pulpit, a theater of the absurd, and revealed religion. Illusion and reality are blurred and meaninglessness displaces meaning. Each candidate denies who he is, and all assume that no one is what he pretends to be.

Political alienation is not a parochial phenomenon. The crisis of confidence documents twenty years of mistrust and alienation, of disillusionment with public policy and elections, and of mistrust of the White House, big business, and the professions. The nation's belief in political effacy is low. More people opt for independence, and fewer trust a party. The electorate is apathetic. Voting appears more meaningless, the state more inaccessable.

Political alienation transforms American politics. It diminishes the significance of party, class, and ideology. It displaces calculations of economics and self-interest with idiosyncratic gut reactions. This change disadvantages the poor, the lower middle class, and the Democratic Party because alienated voters tend to abstain. The party of nonvoters, 30 million habitual abstainers, most of whom are nominal Democrats, is enlarged. Republicans prosper for this reason and because noneconomic and symbolic appeals become more salient.

Mistrust of politics and politicians has additional conservative and irrational effects. Lower-class Democrats rely on the state for succor, yet mistrust the state. Their need for an ideological commitment to the Democratic Party conflicts with their mistrust so that their antipathy to the state nourishes the Republican cry for less government. Many alienated lower-class Democrats, therefore, fail to vote, or vote Republican—that is, contrary to economic self-interest.

Only one caller noted the conservative effect of political alienation.

The most arousing candidates can be the most dangerous. The voting people are missing the point of what to look for, which is choosing candidates of the basis of their class. In the *Herald*—they describe King versus Dukakis as a six pack of beer versus wine and cheese. First, it's wrong, second, it is a slur . . . it's looking at a class breakdown. . . . I don't think King was on the side of the little people. He was on the side of big business people.

Political alienation also lessens the advantage of the incumbent because it may be less damaging to seek office than to have held it. The issue is neither the past nor the future, but the present. It is the campaign, the current Broadway production, that counts. The election contest between two campaigns becomes to theatrical presentations mediated by television. The id of the alienated voter is visceral, immediate, instantaneous.

A political reporter for *The Boston Globe* discussed politics and television with Jerry Williams. "[W]ith a campaign that's this long, you end up voting for candidates based on how good a campaign they ran and you forget about if they were good in office or not. And it's not based on performance in office but performance on the tube."

Widespread corruption is a critical cause of political alienation. But as Yankelovich indicated, the crisis of confidence, the alienation of the electorate, is ultimately a response to the belief that state and society have failed to produce social justice for large numbers. Liberals perceive Ronald Reagan as a practitioner of social injustice, the instigator of a reactionary and inequitable political revival. Concervatives condemn the particularity of the social welfare state. The crisis of confidence, the explosion of mistrust, may be a first encounter in America's battle to redefine priorities. Political alienation is a symptom of national malaise; it affects both public policy and the electoral process.

6

To Catch A Thief

THE alienated voter would like to catch a thief, a political thief—a congressman, a mayor, a state representative, a contractor, a tax examiner—but his pleasure is usually limited to voting against the greater of two evils or not voting. The alienated voter does not evaluate candidates, parties, or platforms according to common standards, nor does he vote primarily in terms of party affiliation, social class, or ideology. His political judgment turns on idiosyncratic, intuitive leaps.

Given this extreme skepticism and the highly personal evaluation of political style, customary political rhetoric and strategy are likely to backfire. The candidate who woos an alienated electorate must avoid the appearance of being a politician, must not conduct opulent campaigns, and must convince alienated voters that he is not corrupt—or at least that he is less corrupt than his opponent. This is not easy to do.

Politicians frequently know that alienated voters are plentiful and that they want information relevant to a candidate's integrity, not his program. The candidate's first response, as we have noted is common-sensical: he proclaims his purity and castigates his opponent. Mud slinging is the common coin designed to purchase the alienated vote. The candidates, however, have not appreciated the subtlety of their problem. There is no reason why alienated voters should believe more in the parry than the thrust.

It's all a pack of lies. You tell me who to believe. You can't. These guys have been lying to the public for so long, and to each other, that they couldn't see the truth if they had

to. Politicians lie. They're supposed to lie. Their business
is to lie. So any amount of bull that will win is OK. I can't
tell who's not lying. Can you?

Speeches, debates, platforms are not believable; the meaning of
party is dissolved by mistrust. Past performance is mitigated by the
belief that no one really knows what politicians do or have done.
The standard cues that once provided meaning and veracity have
been foreclosed. Instead, the candidate's style, hairdo, sweat, wife,
eyes, or shirt indicate the truth behind the false reality. These standard objects of manipulation become the criteria for truth.

Candidates may well know that voters are looking at their eyes
for cues, but they do not know what color their eyes ought to be.
Under these conditions, politicians must construct a new type of
political strategy for the alienated voter. The model may illuminate
the dynamics of a degraded electoral process and political culture.
It may anticipate the future of American politics, and—by contrast—
it might designate the viable elements of genuine democraticpractice.

The bizarre and seemingly irrational choices that we propose are
appropriate for a political system whose fiduciary bond is perceived
as worthless. A peculiar brand of Machiavellianism is necessary for
alienated electorates. The strategic problems are subtle. The issue
is not how to lie and create the illusion of truth; the essential problem of the politics of mistrust is how to tell the truth and make it
credible.

In speculating on possible strategies for winning the alienated
voter, we assume that candidates and voters are rational and selfish;
that is, candidates wish to use their time, money, and manpower
most efficiently, and voters wish to maximize their self-interest.
Voters will estimate and compare benefits they will receive from the
parties. The greater the expected benefits, the more likely a citizen
will vote.

We also assume that alienated voters believe that politicians seek
office not to carry out particular policies, but to reap the rewards of
holding office per se. Politicians treat policies as a means to attain
their private ends, which they can reach only be being elected. Parties
formulate policies to win elections, rather than win elections in order
to formulate policies.

The terms "benefit" and "loss" refer only to the economic or political goals of citizens or parties.[1] Most citizens—at least those who vote—expect benefits if one party is elected, and losses if the other party is elected. The alienated voter expects to lose from the election of either candidate, although he may expect to lose more from the election of one candidate than the other.

Although the United States has the highest rate of nonvoting among viable democracies, a majority of its citizens is committed to the system. They may not believe it is possible to receive all the benefits they think they are entitled to, but they anticipate the possibility of a net gain. This is what makes the political system meaningful to them. Alienated voters, however, structure the available political alternatives in terms of the "lesser of the two evils." Believing that they are denied representation of their interests, they feel alienated, powerless, cynical, cheated.

The rational citizen votes for the party he thinks will provide him with the most benefits during the tenure of the elected official. To do this, he compares the benefits he believes he would have received had the "outs" been in power with the benefits received from the "ins." The difference between these estimates is his expected party differential. A citizen who has an expected party differential of zero expects to benefit or lose the same amount from the election of either candidate. It is rational for a citizen in this situation to abstain. Very few voters believe that they will benefit from the election of both candidates because commitment to one enhances dislike of the opposition.

Several studies of political behavior indicate that citizens tend to pull the candidate they prefer closer to themselves and push the opposition away. They are likely to recall statements made by their favorites, statements that agree with their own views, and compare them to statements of their favorites' opponents, statements that disagree with their own views. This obviously makes the citizens more comfortable with their political choices. The tendency to dislike at least one of the candidates is strengthened by the fact that in America politicians are one of the few culturally legitimate objects of public venom.

The license to release aggression in politics is one of the reasons why politics is such an enjoyable spectator sport. It is possible to receive different kinds of gratification from taking a rational approach toward the lesser of two evils. One source of gratification is the simple fact that the economic or political losses have been minimized. Another source of gratification may stem from the reduction of anger that ensues when one punishes the more evil candidate by voting for his opponent. The alienated voter may savor this pleasure.

Citizens who are committed to the system identify their well-being with at least one of the candidates. This means that they assume that at least some of the statements of their candidate are relevant. Since they interpret the political system in terms of benefits, they may regard the platforms of the candidates as pertinent data, as a relatively reliable indication of what the candidate would do if elected. The alienated do not believe the statements of candidates; they do not regard platforms as reliable indicators of future action. However, if they are to vote they must do so in terms of some criteria that have relevance to their expected losses. Political strategists who seek the alienated vote, or at least, who hope to deflect it, must discover what those criteria are and maximize their values for the alienated voter.

Because the alienated voter discounts the statements of both candidates as equally unattractive, equally unrealistic, and equally meaningless, he is forced to rely on intuitive—and thus, highly personal—feelings. The individuality and randomness of these judgments make the response of the alienated highly unpredictable. This is the strategists' problem. "He looks crooked," is a common response. The question is, how and why does he look crooked, and to whom? No one really knows.

Traditional approaches will not work; in fact, they are likely to backfire. The candidate who seeks the votes of the alienated and who relies on time-honored strategies will be tagged as a traditional politician and will lose. The political game resembles the uncanny bargaining between experienced buyers and sellers of jade, in which unobtrusive measures play a role. Sophisticated sellers of jade estimate the prices that potential buyers are prepared to pay—or not pay—by observing the dilation of their pupils. When potential buyers become aware of this, they cover their eyes with sun glasses. Like the seller of jade, the political strategist seeks arcane signals of the alienated voter's willingness to buy.

The strategist is likely to be more effective by attending to the basic forms of alienation, rather than to the specific stereotypes held by the alienated. Given his pervasive cynicism, the alienated voter tends to vote against the candidate who appears to be more experienced, well known, professional, political, dishonest and heavily financed. These criteria, however, have been developed by the alienated in response to feelings of powerlessness and meaninglessness. The alienated voter, if he responds at all, will respond to the candidate who gives him a sense of power or leads him to believe that the election is meaningful. The problem of wooing the alienated is not simply one of nominating a candidate who does not smoke cigars or who is not fat and pudgy.

Although one can determine the proportion of voters who can be swayed by an appeal to abolish rent control—a concrete issue—we can suggest no method for determining whether a reserved demeanor on television will be interpreted as statesmanlike or vacuous. Modern technology can provide the means to change the color of a candidate's eyes ("I looked in his eyes and I knew he was a crook"); the question still remains: What color should they be? A bold and imaginative style is as likely to succeed as a conservative one. The determinants of strategy are still to be found in the feelings of powerlessness and meaninglessness.

Two strategies are available to the rational candidate who wishes to exploit feelings of powerlessness, and both strategies are advantageous to the party that is out of power. By definition, the incumbent has power and appears to have used it badly, which makes him a significant cause of the alienated's powerlessness. The incumbent cannot exploit the pain he has created. The nonincumbent strategist must convince the alienated voter that if his candidate is elected, the people will recoup their sovereignty. He must attempt this by supplying information that will be taken as meaningful. He will enhance feelings of powerlessness by emphasizing the unchecked tyranny of the incumbents and suggesting that their hegemony is the cause of the citizen's powerlessness. An instructive and dramatic example of this strategy occurred during a gubernatorial election in Massachusetts in the 1960s.

An advertising executive, who had been advising candidates in Massachusetts for thirty years and who wished to take advantage of feelings of political powerlessness, suggested to a high-ranking Republican official that the party would benefit enormously if they placed the following advertisement in newspapers throughout the state:

Negroes
Jews
Protestants
excluded from participation
in
the Democratic Party

The advertising executive understood the explosive character of the advertisement, and was aware of the possibility of an adverse reaction. However, he argued, it would gain many more votes than it would lose because it was essentially true: the Democratic Party traditionally nominated predominantly a Catholic, all-white ticket. The advertisement, in the executive's opinion, would confirm or bring to the surface feelings of powerlessness in alienated Jews, Protestants, and blacks, by identifying the Democratic Party as the cause of their alienation. The effectiveness of this approach would be further heightened by the fact that the Republican slate included an Italian Catholic, a Polish Catholic, a Protestant, a Jew, and a black. In Massachusetts, a coalition-of-minorities strategy that unites Italian Catholics, Protestants, Jews, and blacks can defeat an Irish Catholic candidate. The exploitation of racial and religious antagonisms may be unfortunate, but it is a constant in Massachusetts politics. Given this fact of political life, the Republican nomination of a non-Protestant candidate for governor was obviously a rational strategy, since, for many voters, the religion or the ethnic origin of the candidate is a prime consideration.

The advertising executive's proposal was rejected for two reasons: 1) it might have boomeranged (the Democrats could have pointed to a number of non-Catholics in their party or stressed that the advertisement was un-American); 2) it violated the candidate's sense of "the rules of the game." The former reason is rational, the latter is not unless voters believe in the same rules.

Nevertheless, the gambit is instructive. The man who created this strategy believed that Massachusetts voters—particularly the alienated—were far more sophisticated than most politicians would admit. He insisted that their feelings of powerlessness were well founded and that their image of the political system was basically accurate. This, he argued, is precisely why the old clichés would not work.

The object of the first strategy is to identify the incumbent's party as the cause of the voter's powerlessness. The second strategy offers the alienated voter the possibility of recovery through union with other identified minorities. In such a strategy the candidate emphasizes his own powerlessness; he imputes power to the opposition or perhaps to some power elite (contractors, bookies, big businessmen, labor racketeers). In this "underdog" approach, the candidate suggests that by combining their small increments of power he and the other little people may overthrow the powerful. This call for collaboration offers voters a promise of power and a feeling of participation. The campaign becomes a quest for the Holy Grail of power. The professional politicians who possess the Grail are the mercenary infidels, while the Christians are the little people, the powerless, the penniless, the humble, and the alienated. The rhetoric is not unfamiliar. A speech writer might imagine the following appeal to powerlessness.

> I, too, am an alienated voter. You are not alone. I, too, am a victim of the conspiracy in Beacon Hill and City Hall. I, too, had my political birthright stolen by big business, big builders, big bookies, and big lobbies. The struggle is between the powerful and the powerless. The big guys and us. While Goliath fills high-paying jobs with relatives and friends who don't work, while Goliath exchanges state contracts for campaign contributions, we get highways full of potholes and state buildings that need repair six months after they are built. While Goliath becomes rich and powerful, we live in Taxachusetts. We get clobbered with taxes. And we lose power. Are you as angry as I am?
>
> Join me, David; join me, another little guy, another alienated voter; join your voice with mine in this crusade, and together, we will drive the moneychangers from the temple. With our combined power we are Goliath. We will forge a sword of steel, a rod of righteousness, and we will redeem the birthright given to us by the Founding Fathers.

This strategy not only takes advantage of the alienated voter's feelings of powerlessness by offering him power, it also offers him a way to believe that elections can have meaning. This approach creates a meaningful bond between apparently powerless candidates and powerless voters; it promises a paradise of political power, redemption, and justice.

For example, in 1960, when John Collins, a maverick candidate for mayor of Boston, opposed John Powers, the powerful president of the state Senate and a veteran "pol," Collins, the amateur and the nonprofessional, restricted to a wheelchair, campaigned on the slogan: "Stop power politics—elect a hands free mayor." Whenever possible he referred to his organization as a "small group of enthusiastic amateurs" at war with an army of mercenaries. He also sponsored an essay contest to define "power politics." The winning essay, submitted by a fourteen-year-old girl, defined a power politician as "a man who is surrounded by political bigwigs and who administers to his and their gains first, and to the people not at all." One Collins supporter stated, "I don't like the idea that since all the big guys are for Powers, the little people like us should be for him too."

This David and Goliath strategy is not new to American politics. It is, in part, a reflection of the culture's disdain for politicians. Michael Dukakis, twice governor of Massachusetts and widely reputed for his honesty and virtue, used this strategy in 1982 and won. Dukakis enriched his "David" by appearing as a humble, repentent candidate, sobered by defeat, who had learned his lesson.

I've learned a lot since I've been out of office. The first and most important thing I learned is not to take your vote for granted and I hope my campaign this time has proved to you that I've learned the lesson you taught me very well. I need your help and I'm asking for your vote. And, if you give me your support this Tuesday, and we are successful in November, we can put this state together again. The task will not be easy . . . to take Massachusetts in a new direction, to replace the special interests with public interests, and to restore honesty to a government that is reeling with corruption, I need your help this Tuesday.

[Announcer:] Mike Dukakis. To get Massachusetts working—again—honestly. Paid for by the Dukakis Committee.

This advertisement, the centerpiece of a radio campaign, portrayed Dukakis as a little person in need of the help of other little people. The state, like Humpty Dumpty, can be put together again, but only if the little people join with their little leader. Their joining is the precondition for a return of their power. The governor makes this offer more meaningful by suggesting, unlike many professional politicians that the task will not be easy—a sober and realistic message that resonates with alienated views. Dukakis strengthened his credibility by arguing that the Commonwealth must replace the special interests with the public interest. The agenda of the alienated, in other words, is the agenda of democracy. The interests of the candidate and his alienated constituency converge: he and they are one.

Common sense suggests that since powerlessness is the most salient attribute of alienation, strategists should exploit this painful feeling. However, more promising strategies may be developed to take advantage of feelings and meaninglessness. Meaninglessness may be experienced in two ways. A citizen may feel that an election is without meaning because there are no real differences between the candidates, or he may feel that a rational decision is impossible because the information he needs is lacking. If the candidates and platforms are very similar or identical, or if the voter refuses to give credence to campaign promises because he thinks the candidates are dishonest, it will be difficult to find meaningful information on which to base a voting decision.

A strategy that offers the alienated voter information he did not expect to receive may take advantage of feelings of meaninglessness. The alienated voter regards as meaningful information on the size and source of campaign expenditures, because he believes that an opulent campaign indicates that contributors own the candidate and that the public interest is foreclosed by private power.

In 1962, a candidate in the Democratic gubernatorial primary in Massachusetts, who was completely unknown to the general public, made explicit use of this strategy. The candidate undoubtedly hoped that his name, John F. (Francis) Kennedy, was in itself a meaningful message. Kennedy, the unknown, notified the public that he would not pay for television or radio time, newspaper advertisements, billboards, bumper stickers, or any other form of publicity that required money. That he did not appear on television or advertise in any other medium made his claim credible. With one stroke, he satisfied the syllogism of the alienated voter: Expensive campaigning is the cause of the candidate's indebtedness to his contributors; Kennedy's campaign is frugal; therefore, Kennedy is not indebted. Kennedy's strategy, however, may have been self-defeating for those voters who were unaware of his candidacy.

This noncampaign strategy is revealing. It works by negating traditional strategies. It is the ultimate inversion, an appeal on the assumption that everything political is debased. This negation is appropriate for a political world that is profoundly antipolitical and deeply alienated.

Endicott Peabody, a former governor of Massachusetts, also appealed to meaninglessness, but in quite a different way. The bizarre quality of his strategy and that of the John Kennedy who took the vow of poverty illustrate how an alienated electorate promotes bizarre campaigning.

During a primary election in the 1960s, Endicott Peabody developed a meaningful strategic gambit. Peabody sponsored a number of five-minute "news" broadcasts called the *Political Roundup*. The format of the program was similar to that of any television news roundup; it consisted of a number of news clips dealing with international and national events interspersed with clips of Peabody campaigning. The announcer, a hired employee of the Peabody organization, "reported" a groundswell for Peabody—which was, in fact, the case. Although *Political Roundup* was preceded and followed by the legally required statement that the broadcast is sponsored by the Peabody for Governor Committee," the advertisement appeared to be a regularly scheduled program—that is, a news report of the Peabody groundswell. Since it appeared to be nonsponsored or nonpolitical, it might have been meaningful to alienated voters. One Boston television station discontinued *Political Roundup* because, in the words of the manager, it "confused" many voters.

Political Roundup was a complex deception. The news content was essentially accurate: pollsters' data did indicate a groundswell for Peabody. But because that information appeared to be partisan its legitimacy had to be underscored by presenting it in an apparently objective news report. Campaigning for the alienated voter is hazardous. The spoken word and its accepted meaning are no longer credible to him. Communications, however, may contain latent as well as manifest messages, private implied meanings as well as public obvious ones. The Kennedys, who did not take a vow of poverty, became masters of a scheme involving a deluge of data. A candidate like John Fitzgerald Kennedy, who can spout facts and figures that are allegedly supported by graphs and tables, a candidate who can demonstrate a wide and detailed grasp of international and local matters, may create the impression of being a statesman and a scholar. In other words, a nonpolitician, a dispenser of meaningful information. The deluge of data, however, is often not presented for purposes of informing voters. The data may well be accurate, informative, and a meaningful aid for understanding the issues, but this is not why it is featured; the strategy is designed to enhance the image of the candidate. The enlightenment of the electorate is not the principal aim.

The Kennedy braintrust understood the significance of image to a mistrustful electorate. In 1962, Edward Kennedy, at the time politically unsophisticated, ran for the U.S. Senate. Many knew that his bid for office was nepotistic. His candidacy was a pseudoevent much in need of legitimization. The braintrust opted for the deluge of data approach. They prepped the candidate with question-and-answer sessions to fill the gaps in his sparse education. A member of the Kennedy braintrust described its approach to the alienated.

> He must sell himself not only as a vigorous person, but also as a person of intelligence, particularly in Massachusetts where people have demanded much more of their senators and their governors than they have of other office holders. So it's a question of presenting the candidate in a mature and sophisticated way . . . giving more formal speeches, giving speeches in depth, discussing issues on a semi-academic level, not so much to educate the people on the issues or convince them of the virtue of the issues or his knowledge of the issues, but broadly to show the person that this is a young man of intelligence. My specific advice in a number of cases has been to talk above the audience. That is, for some candidates this might not be the correct approach—to talk over your audience's head. But in this particular case, and under the circumstances that Kennedy is working under, a highly sophisticated presentation to an audience above their level makes good sense, and is good campaign strategy.

The candidacy of Edward Kennedy employed a strategy designed to exploit feelings of meaninglessness. Alienated voters want candidates they perceive as nonpoliticians, candidates free of obligations, free of the need to steal, and free to work for the public good. Who fits this role? Beautiful People: people of independent means; people of class and substance; people of high social status, old money, and old family; people who transcend the corrosive effects of competition and the meanness of reality; people who ski in Chile, sail the Mediterranean, winter in Aspen and Palm Springs, and summer in Hyannis and Newport. Celebrities may qualify: movie stars, the enormously rich, astronauts—men and women whose celebrity, or wealth, or social status removes them from the temptations of crass materialism. Their otherworldliness frees them from bourgeois hunger and permits them to indulge in an ethic of public service. Horatio Alger's hero is no longer the role model.

For Americans, these Beautiful People are ego ideals; they are the fulfillment of the American Dream. If they happen to be handsome and glamorous, all the better. Their political prominence is a symptom of the low estate of American politics. Social class, old money, and celebrity become more meaningful when politics as a profession becomes more hateful. Americans often select leaders who epitomize the success of the system but whose virtue lies in the fact that they need have nothing to do with it. Their cleanliness and apoliticality becomes redemptive, particularly during crises of confidence.

Another effective strategy to take advantage of feelings of meaninglessness is the appeal of frankness. In this strategy, the candidate tells the voter many facts of political life that are usually censored, but that the alienated voter has discovered independently. This is the strongest evidence possible to establish the candidate's integrity. For example, the candidate could boldy state that campaigns require organization and that party workers demand patronage in return for services. He could read the names of suspect campaign contributors—for instance, contractors. He could recite the indictments and convictions of the incumbent's appointees. He could list the members of the families of state and city employees who are the beneficiaries of nepotism. He could point out that these are the facts of political life for all candidates. In other words, he could repeat the alienated voter's analysis of the distribution of power and privilege. Having established himself as frank and open, he could then go on to differentiate himself from his opponent.

More ingenious gambits designed to take advantage of meaninglessness can be imagined. The alienated voter believes that the candidates take care of themselves and their entourage rather than the public. Any information indicating that the candidate cares about voters would appear meaningful, providing that it also appears non-partisan. During the elections we have observed, candidates spent large amounts of money proclaiming their virtues. It might have been more rational to spread this message by more indirect and imaginative means.

The candidate, for example, could send voluntary workers to conduct an opinion poll among the alienated. Since the poll would not have the usual academic objectives, the sample would be chosen for political rather than statistical criteria. The pollster would tell the respondent that the purpose of the poll is to inform candidate X about the desires of the electorate. The ulterior purpose would be to show the respondent that the candidate is interested in his welfare. The incontrovertible evidence that the candidate has spent time and money attempting to find out how the voter feels can be meaningful in the assessment of the candidate's character. As a byproduct, the data may furnish the candidate with useful information, but the principal purpose has been accomplished the moment the interview is completed.

The great majority of strategists respond to an alienated constituency in a most simple-minded and counterproductive way. They attack and counterattack. The problem, however, is that the public has no proof of a candidate's virtue. More subtle strategies should be introduced. A candidate's honor may be affirmed if he can introduce issues with a powerful moral dimension, issues that relate to how the good life is supposed to be lived, issues totally unlike those that politicians typically advance. Ronald Reagan and the new right have introduced such issues: pornography, abortion, capital punishment, drunken driving, and school prayer. A shrewd caller, commenting on the 1982 gubernatorial contest in Massachusetts, suggested that King could win easily if he concentrated on "moral issues." "But once conservatives get on the moral issues, he picked up points galore. . . . he'll clobber the Republican, if he concentrates on pornography, drinking, and that stuff. If he tries to concentrate on politics, what he's done in office . . . he's gonna lose."

The inference is that moral issues transcend the traditional political agenda. The spokesman has a higher morality, a vision of life's possibilities, and is surely not engaged in political brokerage. The stra-

tegic advantages of ethical preachment in an alienated electorate are
large. Ronald Reagan aptly demonstrated this. The conservative host
understood this.

> Dukakis makes the whole thrust of his campaign the cor-
> ruption issue and eventually the King people were able
> to turn the attention of the electorate to other issues,
> such as capital punishment, drunk driving, abortion, and
> when people started looking at these issues, what you
> might call the visceral conservatism of the electorate was
> aroused.

The caller who originally raised the question of moral issues in
campaigning understands their diversionary role.

> The same thing, I think, is with Reagan, President Reagan.
> If he stays on his record, the people who supported him,
> the congressmen, senators who supported him are going
> to get clobbered. But once you get on abortion and other
> things like that (he came out with a law and order pro-
> gram Saturday). I think he is going to pick up some
> seats.

The strategy of supporting moral issues can provide a sense of
meaning to alienated voters. The Congress and state legislatures are
concerned with bread and butter issues that deal with the distribution
of dollars and cents to competing constituencies. For the alienated
voter, dollars and their distribution are the medium of corruption.
Moral issues, even when politicized, are not perceived as traditionally
political. They may involve the expenditure of millions of dollars,
but the moralized objective of the expenditure is not so readily perceived as the product of crass of political bargaining. The preachment
of moral issues during the campaign may be taken as a signal that
the candidate is on the high road. The ethical crusader stands in
sharp contrast to the wheeler-dealer. The moral majority is not merely
a veiled religious reference, it is a part of a political strategy designed
to take advantage of cultural as well as political alienation.

   The problem with this strategy is that issues of lifestyle are sharply
divisive. Unlike bread and butter issues, which tend to divide Dem-

ocrats and Republicans along party lines, and which are negotiable, moral issues cut across party lines and class divisions and are non-negotiable. One cannot compromise with good and evil. Though a position strongly favoring abortion may attract some of the alienated, it may also repel alienated voters who do not favor abortion.

An additional strategy to take advantage of alienation caused by a sense of political meaninglessness is endorsement by or identification with a generally admired nonpolitical person. In this common strategy, the candidate is endorsed by a well-known and highly legitimized ego ideal, such as Walter Cronkite or Farrah Fawcett, on the assumption that the celebrity will add luster to the candidate. The strategist assumes that charisma is transferable: love Sinatra, love Reagan. Although the magical thinking involved here is particularly appealing to the people of North America, the problem is that the alienated may love the pure and nonpolitical Farrah, but perceive her political tag-along as contaminated. Mistrust diffuses the transference.

The endorsement strategy can, however, be deftly executed. During the 1982 gubernatorial campaign, Paul Corsetti, a reporter for the *Boston Herald*, was sentenced to serve ninety days in jail because he refused to comply with a court order requiring him to name the sources for a story concerning an alleged murder. Corsetti became an instant hero in the tradition of his predecessor Sam Adams: another defender of the freedom of the press. Governor Edward King, whose administration was pockmarked with convictions and rumors of quid pro quo, had a marvelous opportunity to recoup the alienated vote through his power to commute Corsetti's sentence or free him. The governor commuted Corsetti's sentence to four days, the amount of time he had already served. Aligning himself with another King, the governor used the endorsement strategy.

Did you hear on the news about Paul Corsetti, The *Herald American* reporter who refused to name his sources during a murder trial and was sentenced to jail for ninety days for contempt of court? When he asked the governor for a pardon, and in refusing Governor King said, "I am a firm supporter of the law. You broke the law by committing a crime, therefore I will not pardon you. But you broke the law out of conscience and because of your prin-

ciples and personal beliefs, not out of greed or self interest. I respect you for that. And, out of compassion for you
and your family, I'll commute your sentence to the time
you've already served."

Governor King then quoted the Reverend Martin Luther
King, Jr.

I submit that an individual who breaks a law that conscience tells him is unjust, and willingly accepts the penalty
by staying in jail to arouse the conscience of the community over its injustice, is, in reality, expressing the highest respect for the law.

Governor King appears to be the antithesis of the professional
"pol." He supports the law. As a man of principle, he abhors greed
and self-interest. But he has conscience and compassion, a sense of
right and justice; he identifies himself with Martin Luther King. To
temper justice with mercy is not the common course of Massachusetts
politicians.

The construction of political strategies to engage the alienated voter
is a realistic, though sad, enterprise. It may be playful and entertaining, but it is an enterprise appropriate to a political system in
disarray. The manipulative strategy is a rational response to crises
of confidence. The degradation of democracy is the real issue. A
long history of public corruption poisons every facet of the political
process. Public policy becomes private interest, political campaigns
replicate the duplicity of public life, the outcome of elections matters
little, fund-raising becomes bribery, politics becomes business, nepotism replaces merit, and quid pro quo prevents the rational allo-
cation of scarce resources. The manipulative strategies designed to
lure the alienated voter are perfectly normal in a political world where
manipulation and mistrust are the norms.

The strategies are duplicitous in many ways. Ultimately they are
intended to take advantage of voters. The deluge of data, for example,
is designed to impress, not inform; the public opinion poll is not
designed to elicit public opinion but to manipulate it. These are
petty deceits. They degrade public life. But they are responses to a

degraded public life. In this sad cycle, politics becomes what it is assumed to be: a web of deceit.

Crises of confidence, however, might be a natural and perhaps healthy response to political decay, a cathartic withdrawal of support, a major shift of public opinion that signals the emergence of a new constituency. Crises of confidence may create the conditions for progressive reform or reaction. The historical setting in which they occur will largely determine their effect, an issue we will deal with presently.

Twenty years of mistrust began to abate during the second and third years of Mr. Reagan's incumbency. Public opinion pollsters reported that Americans, in large numbers, were beginning to trust the president and the political system, and were beginning to feel more confident about their personal lives and their futures. Patriotism became the order of the day as Mr. Reagan reaffirmed the apocalyptic dangers of that "evil empire," the Soviet Union. The Punch and Judy show in Grenada promoted a patriotic orgy, as did the Iranian hostage crisis. Both incidents were real, but they were also triumphs of public relations. The economy improved and the bourgeois hunger of Americans was fed by the president's constant reminder of the cornucopia available to those who honor the Prostestant ethic.

Was the crisis of confidence an extended but superficial malaise? Could a profound failure of trust be so quickly evaporated by political artifice, promises of redemption, comic military adventurism, and improvement in some of the major economic indicators? The basic commitment to free enterprise and liberal politics continued during the crisis. The ultimate faith was not corroded by heresy. Was the crisis a peripheral and time-bound response to an unusual series of shocks, an alienation not likely to be repeated?

The evidence suggests that the crisis of confidence was a response to several unusual sets of circumstances but that it was also a grandiose and skeptical inquiry into some basic American values. Will the confidence gap of the 1960s and 1970s be viewed in the 1990s as a precursor for some future transvaluation of values? Should supply-side economics fail and stagflation again become a reality, the crisis of confidence may enter its second stage.

Deep structural contradictions exist below the prosperous surface of American life, contradictions that, if unresolved, could ignite the second stage. The budget deficit, the adverse balance of payments, the growth of poverty, the steady rate of unemployment, the low rate of growth, the deindustrialization of America, and the inability of the nation to compete successfully in world markets could encourage severe economic hardship. Would the American consensus withstand a prolonged downturn of the economy?

There are many plausible scenarios for the future of American politics. The problem is to construct one that is realistic.

Note

1. Anthony Downs, *An Economic Theory of Democracy* (New York: Harper and Brothers, 1957).

7

Liberal Language and the Failure of Class Consciousness

Talk radio participants, during the years of the crisis of confidence, complained bitterly of crime in the streets, indifferent police, and gouging landlords. They referred to politicians as crooks and liars, elections as meaningless exercises, and big business as the despoiler of the environment. Essentially they were complaining that atomism betrayed eighteenth-century liberal social ideals. They suffered acutely the isolation and loneliness of everyday life, and the absence of fellowship among neighbors and between political trustees and citizens. This is the alienation of urban life for which talk radio is the poignant vehicle.

Atomism, this experience of aloneness and impotence, was tapped by the survey research that documented the crisis. The pollsters, however, did not analyze the quality of daily life in neighborhoods, the locus of the most profound social alienation, nor did they sample the political pathology engendered by state and local politics, the fear of being mugged, the incivility of salespeople, the brutality of policemen, and the drug culture at high schools. Talk radio documents the personal and local exchanges that constitute the immediate and concrete context of experience. In these experiences the crisis of the bourgeois ethic is most poignantly felt; here the fracturing of communities energizes isolation, fear and powerlessness—the roster of alienation. This alienation might have led to some movement for social change, since such change is often possible when social problems are perceived in ethical terms. If nothing else—and there were many more scandals at both national and local levels—Watergate and Abscam confirmed the belief that ethical degeneration had become an American problem.

Many public opinion surveys reveal that a substantial minority of Americans turned away from the models of the big businessman and the political leader, and instead offered their esteem to professions that were perceived as nonpolitical and underrewarded: scientists, clergymen, scholars, and so on. These of course, are professions whose members proclaimed their moral leadership during the controversy over the Vietnam War. Practitioners of these professions, apparently nonpolitical and unattached to big business, seemed to the radio respondents to have escaped the bondage of self-interest and the temptations of crass materialism.

For many Americans, the Horatio Alger pursuit of self-realization in a society that rewards honesty and initiative, the idea of equality before the law, indeed the ideal of democracy itself—in short, many of the elements that constitute the American Dream—were seen as a myth. Public opinion polls taken between 1965 and 1981 tend to bear this out. Since 1964 the Center for Political Studies at the University of Michigan has asked respondents: "Would you say that the government is pretty much run by a few big interests looking out for themselves, or that it is run for the benefit of all people?" In 1964, 29 percent agreed; sixteen years later, 70 percent agreed. By the time Mr. Reagan was elected, less than one-third of the sample believed that the state fulfilled its fiduciary responsibility. More than half of those queried in the late 1970s believed that the government did not know what it was doing. During those decades, a majority of Americans believed that the tax laws were written to benefit the rich, not the average man.

During the crisis, political scandal was no longer taken as aberrant, but rather as symptomatic of widespread political corruption. Quid pro quo and nepotism were taken as common coin of state and local politics. The picture that emerges is a battleground of self-interest, in which powerful political insiders triumph at the expense of the common man. The reality of oligarchy and class negated the myth of democracy and equality. The American public felt victimized by a maldistribution of social justice.

Twenty years of mistrust produced some skepticism and some political change. The Democratic Party, as incumbent during the crisis, fell victim to the alienation of the epoch that it had generated. The national perception of endless inversions of the proper order provided an appropriate setting for the advancement of someone so apparently out of the mainstream of American politics as Mr. Reagan, someone who identified the state as the source of excess and abuse. Ronald Reagan was the beneficiary of this crisis. Much of his world view is a mirror image of the more primitive aspects of the crisis.

A more significant outcome of the crisis may be the creation of long-term positive attitudes toward social justice, welfare rights, and equal economic opportunity—a posture that will survive the current administration and its efforts to curtail social welfare. Still, this hardly amounts to anything in the way of social or political change.

Despite some achievements in the vindication of social justice—the effort to terminate the Vietnam War, for example, was surely one of the great triumphs of popular sovereignty—two decades of mistrust and a pervasive national loss of confidence in politics, big business, and the professions produced remarkably little change. There was no national effort to politicize mistrust or to form a third party; nor were there serious attempts to infiltrate and move either major party. There was no significant breakthrough in political thought, no large-scale demand for qualitative change, no heightened socialist awareness, and no cry for a socialist party.

Ironically, in working to support Reagan, the crisis set the stage for a massive revival of the values of which millions were skeptical during the crisis. Supply-side economics places tremendous emphasis on the virtues of eighteenth-century liberalism, the beneficent effect of self-interest and accumulation, and the satisfactions of material comfort. After twenty years of doubt, Americans were more committed to liberal virtues and more involved with the bourgeois ethic than they had been since the 1920s. America's liberal unanimity survived the crisis.

The crisis of confidence was a lost opportunity to create some enlightened criticism of America and some social change. But other critical periods in American history—and there have been few in this culture of confidence—also failed to produce alternatives, biting social thought, or anything out of the eighteenth-century liberal ordinary. The great age of reform, the age of Populism, and the New Deal produced little new or trenchant in political thought. It seems that the absence of creative political ideas is an American tradition.

Despite the consciousness-raising that occurred during the 1960s and 1970s, despite the public's claim of moral decay in business and in government, despite the ethical framework in which social distress was set, the political understanding of the alienated, as represented by talk radio respondents, remained unsophisticated. Their criticism was hemmed in by old emotional commitments to free enterprise and electoral politics; their understanding of politics lacked a sense of cause and effect. The angry public had global and undetailed knowledge—a collage of newspaper and television reports of a few major events—interpreted through a prism of mistrust. There was no quantification, no discretion.

The alienated may sense the inversions of politics—the role reversals and grotesqueries, the breaking of fiduciary bonds, for example—but they seem to have no idea that the media legitimize the power structure and the culture. The idea that political reality may be a crafted illusion usually escapes them. They have little sense that public education is a major conduit of political socialization, a vehicle for reinforcing class stratification. The alienated criticize the effects of self-interest and materialism, yet fail to understand that capitalism facilitates both of those. The overwhelming majority of Americans both love free enterprise and are skeptical of self-interest, but they have practically no understanding that free enterprise is self-interest unleashed, that self-interest is the motive that makes free enterprise work. It is as if the system and its parts were discrete entities; as if self-interest and accumulation were metaphysical niceties not rooted in any material substratum.

While disgruntled Americans are convinced that the policies of big business are antithetical to the public good and that big business exploits the public, opinion polls indicate that Americans are overwhelmingly committed to free enterprise. More than 90 percent of Americans believe that free enterprise has served America marvelously well and that it is the best way a nation can organize its economic life. Disturbed by selfishness, skeptical of big business, Americans nevertheless embrace the idea of free enterprise as if it were a separate entity. Americans may question manifestations of the traditional liberal tenet, but they remain committed to that tenet.

The liberal conviction insists that the system and its basic institutions (e.g., free enterprise and electoral politics) bear no responsibility for the sorrows of the nation. The beliefs of the Founding Fathers, complemented by the triumph of capitalism, are the core of our political religion. The American way forces critics to analyze political and economic problems without ever defining them as systemic.

The crisis of confidence supplies us with many examples of the illusoriness of this diagnosis: top management may blunder or misappropriate funds, but the corporation itself is regarded as sound; congressmen on the make, mayors who grant abatements for cash, apparatchiks in the White House, and bureaucrats are mistrusted, but not the government of the States of America or the American way. A dichotomy exists in the public mind between the institutions and the leadership—between Madison's countervailing powers and the machinations of Boss Tweed and presidents Harding, Nixon, and their epigones: corruptors who upset this delicate balance. The CIA's role in the Bay of Pigs crisis and the Watergate plumbers, for example, were perceived as wrong, even dangerous. Both Kennedy and Nixon were attacked for promoting immoral activity. But these were considered personal errors on the part of the executives; they were not seen as deriving from a total political structure. A president may err, but the presidency must remain beyond reproach. To take another example, Jimmy Carter was reviled and lost an election, but the policies that precipitated the Iran hostage crisis continued unquestioned in the succeeding administration. Problems result from the fact that a good system has been abused by bad men who broke the rules, not from any systemic malfunction. This was also the theory advanced by Progressives and New Dealers. The bosses and their machines, with the complicity of recently arrived immigrants, corrupted urban democratic political institutions, and so Progressives turned their talents to elminiating bad machines. Franklin Roosevelt in the midst of our greatest depression, always argued that his task was to restore the integrity of the capitalist system. On no occasion did he argue that the free enterprise system had malfunctioned: it was always the "minions of great wealth" who were to blame. The system remained unsullied. But Roosevelt went further than this. He argued that the Great Depression was not even an American tragedy, but a reaction to European troubles. The system again remained pure. The Great Depression, the Watergate scandal, and the Vietnam War may have fostered crises of confidence, but those crises never became crises of legitimacy.

American political style discourages systemic criticism. That style, working within party structure, accommodates conservatives and liberals alike. Because there is no radical disruption from within, confrontation is contained, and this encourages the public to believe that the American political system works and works well. The chaos of the Chicago Democratic convention in 1968, highly publicized as it was, led to no significant reordering of party structure. In a sense, this stance of the American public is consistent with the timidity of American political theorists, whose work has been largely to patch together a system set out in the eighteenth century. America has produced no significant radical political theorist—a Rousseau, say, or a Marx—who undertakes to criticize the political system itself. This absence means that there is no serious challenge to the status quo. Even in the depth of the Great Depression, when Americans were paying some attention to leftist ideas, no strong challenge came out of those ideas, either in the form of a radical party or of a radical rhetoric.

Essentially the rhetoric, the political language of our country, is the language of eighteenth-century liberalism. Liberal language assumes the sanctity of private property, the largeness of opportunity, the importance of class and class conflict. Liberal rhetoric postulates the need for compromise and incrementalism. The temper is pragmatic and optimistic—a testament to bourgeois stability. The vocabulary of large-scale change and revolution is absent. The subtle language of social despair is also unavailable—alienation, reification, false consciousness. Liberal language can grasp concensus politics but it can not imagine a transcendent perspective or the means to create a new world. That language serves both Democrats and Republicans well.

In matters of particular detail (abortion, gay rights, and so on), our right-wing and left-wing talk show hosts disagree. But they have no language to go beyond the superficial disagreement; apart from the sides they take on an issue, they sound the same. The phrase, so fashionable now, "to talk about the issues," becomes a weapon in a conflict over style—not, certainly, over substance. It is not surprising that talk show callers, complaining about crime in the streets or drugs in the schools, think they are talking about the issues; but they support no significant change in the political system.

This narrowness of political thinking on the part of talk radio respondents reflects the general tendency of the American public to encourage conventional political behavior. Talk radio callers, worried about crime in the streets, for example, vote out the incumbent and vote in a president who says he will wipe out street crime. As long as a voting public sees its situation only in terms of particular details in the social fabric, elections will mean, at most, changes of individual personalities. And there lies the danger. A public that has no grasp of the radical responsibilities of politics is all too vulnerable to irrational fear of specific events and—corollary and more dangerous—to worshiping a personality who promises to control specific events. Lurking behind the fears of the callers—fears that are encouraged by the biases of the hosts—are dark pathological areas that need only the prodding of a forceful individual to burst into destructive flame. Today the public may want to get drugs out of the schools; tommorrow a charismatic leader may get that public to wipe out the Jews or the Hispanics or the Asians who supposedly bring those drugs to the schools. If we listen to the voices on our radios, we can hear the urgency of a people struggling to believe in an eighteenth-century idea and to make it work in a multiethnic, multisocial, polyglott, twentieth-century society.

Postscript: Nagasaki, Mon Amour

O N September 9, 1982, Avi Nelson interviewed Major General Charles Sweeney, United States Air Force Retired. General Sweeney was the pilot of the Air Force crew that dropped the atomic bomb on Nagasaki on August 9, 1945. Since that time increasing numbers of Americans have come to regard the dropping of that bomb and the one that razed Hiroshima as different from conventional acts of war; They see the use of atomic bombs as a crime against humanity, as a new dimension in international immorality. But this view is not that of the majority who, in 1945 and now, see the bombings as hastening the end of the war and saving countless American lives. General Sweeney and his talk show host are part of that majority.

Nelson welcomed the general and asked about the newspaper accounts of airmen who had served in his command and became emotionally ill. General Sweeney denied the stories and, like a civic leader, set out the business and professional accomplishments of his military colleagues. Though one suffered a severe nervous breakdown, the others prospered. In fact, many of them took advantage of their military training when seeking civilian employment; their military credentials were an advantage in seeking employment in the highly competitive world of military procurement.

The men of Sweeney's squadron were portrayed as modest and productive middle-class figures. They were not adversely affected by the moral questions that nag the idea of nuclear warfare. The general's affirmation of his colleagues' well-being impressed the host.

So the conventional stories that we hear about people—totally untrue. And the newspapers did it simply to sell

newspapers. And there have been some exposés, but they didn't get as much publicity as the first one.

Indeed, according to the general the members of the crew that bombed Nagasaki saw that mission as a cause for celebration and remembrance. They remained close comrades. General Sweeney reported on their most recent reunion. "We had a reunion two weeks ago in Seattle. I wasn't able to make it because I was in Europe, but the guys had a ball." The host, entirely sympathetic, said, "I was going to ask if the guys ever got together." "Absolutely," responded General Sweeney, "it's going to be in 1984 in Philadelphia, is our next reunion." (Though nearly forty years had passed since 1945, and the crew were men in their sixties and seventies, they were still "guys" in this talk show dialogue.)

This image of middle American folksiness and good will was reinforced by a curious domestic note. A woman telephoned and addressed General Sweeney.

I'd like to ask General Sweeney some questions. Was his children affected or is affected in any way. And, also if he's free tonight, I'd like to ask him out to dinner.

Host, guest, and caller laughed uproariously. The general accepted the invitation, laughed again, and remarked: "The first question, were my children affected? No, I don't think so."

The host probed:

Are you talking in the medical sense, because of the radiation, or are you talking in the psychological sense for being the children of a father who dropped the bomb or went on the bombing mission?

GENERAL: No, I would say they are quite healthy. My daughter, Marilyn, lives in Marshfield. I have another daughter who lives in Connecticut. You might know she is married to a state police officer, Trooper Howe, Marilyn Howe.

CALLER: Oh, yes, I know her quite well.

GENERAL: Oh, you do?

CALLER: Yes, I'm her sister.

GENERAL, [laughing]: Get off the air. That's my daughter.

HOST: I was suspicious when she asked you out to dinner tonight.

GENERAL: The only thing with the children is that they have a proclivity for practical jokes.

CALLER: Yes, we take after our father.

The Sweeney family was shown to be playful and close; and Avi Nelson wanted to know more about the family. He asked if the children were affected by their father's participation in the bombing of Nagasaki.

Well, before you go, the question you asked . . . I know because your father's here, you have to be real concerned about the answer. The question you asked is one that I think a lot of people would like to have a serious answer to. Medically, I assume there was nothing.

No problems with any of the children really.

Psychologically, did you ever have any difficulties with other kids at school or when the politics got a little tough?

No.

Were there ever any feelings or misgivings about your father having been the pilot?

No, it seemed like the kids in school looked up to him. They looked at it like he was a hero and stuff, and that was hard for us in some ways to accept because we looked at him as our father.

So, he was better off with the other kids, is what you're saying? (laughter)

Father and daughter confirmed the popular image of the crew and their families: decent, unexceptional "guys" who were proud of each other and of their country.

General Sweeney interrupted the conversation, laughed, and objected, "I don't know, that was a kind of compliment, Michele. Being a father is real fun with you guys." His daughter affirmed, "Yeah, he was just a regular father. Nobody else knew the difference and so forth." Avi Nelson concluded, "So it, never affected you." "No, never at all, whatsoever."

General Sweeney's daughter presented the image of a solid, fun-loving caring family, the father of whom might be a businessman or professional, a nondescript, thoroughly decent parent. There was nothing unusual about this family: no moral compunction, no sadness, no stigma, no senseof having participated in anything extraordinary. The bombing of Nagasaki was, in fact, taken as a hero's work.

In his conversation with Nelson, General Sweeney did not appear to have seen anything problematic in his historic mission. In his view, the bombing was not only strategically sound for America, but was also an act of salvation for the Japanese, a people, according to the general—speaking without irony—noted for their brutality and their politeness.

Sixteen people phoned General Sweeney. Two were obliquely concerned with the morality of releasing an atomic weapon; the remainder were interested in the technical problems involved in delivering and exploding the bomb. One moralist speculated about the response of the Japanese.

I'm wondering if the Japanese people have ever really accepted it, as an act of war, or is it a deep scar, similar to the feelings of the black people in this nation? Is it something that maybe we'll never get rid of over there in Japan?

This is General Sweeney. I'd like to answer that. I guess you can tell my voice from Avi's. Two years ago in Washington, D.C., I met the president of Sanyo, a man named Sumyo Shimoda. He was there for our reunion in Washington, D.C. He came all the way with the mayor of Hiroshima and part of his staff just to be with us at our reunion. And we laughed, and we joked, and we talked, and he said to me "Perhaps someday you will come to Japan."

I didn't have any special plan, but last year I went to Tokyo. I telephoned him in Hiroshima, which is 500 miles from Tokyo and he said, "How soon can you leave?" And I was at Yokoto airbase and I said, "In two hours." And he sent his car out to pick me up, and ensconced me in the most beautiful suite in the Imperial Hotel, which is the finest in the world, I think, certainly one of the finest, overlooking the Imperial Gardens, and so forth. And I was his guest for five days—I got embarrassed—or six days. And I was treated royally.

He said, "You know, I was a twelve-year-old boy in Hiroshima. And I was in a bomb shelter and they had an air raid." So, he said, "I just came out and just as I did, I saw these strange parachutes." He said, "I ducked down again and just as I ducked down, the bomb went off." And, strangely, he had seen those parachutes and, of course, there was trauma and shock, but he was not injured. And he was then twelve years old. And he said to me, "You know, after we reflected on the thing, we concluded that we love you Americans." This is Mr. Shimoda talking to me in Tokyo. He said, "We love you Americans because you wanted to save as many of us as you could and Tojo wanted to kill us all."

General Sweeney used this remarkable story to suggest that the Japanese have not only forgiven the Americans, but even view the bombing as good or, at least, as the lesser of two evils. General Sweeney's remarks, and those of most callers, disregarded the apocalyptic nature of the bombing and saw it as an ordinary act of war, just another strategic decision.

General Sweeney was on the air for more than an hour. The discussion rarely dealt with the effects of the bomb. Most callers were interested in the technical and scientific problems involved in building and delivering the bomb. Oddly enough, several callers were interested in the weather and its effect on the mission.

I don't have a question about leather, but about weather. What was the cloud cover like on August 9, 1945, over Nagasaki?

Over Nagasaki was 6/10–8/10 puffy summer clouds; at base 8,000, at tops about 10.

So you could see the target?

We made our approach by radar, which was verboten according to instructions but we were also running out of fuel. So, I decided to make the approach by radar. The radar operator, Sergeant Buckley, gave what we call the rate and drift corrections to Captain Beecham, the bombardier, over the intercom. Beecham had the bomb site all lined up on the target, did get a break in the clouds and released.

He [Professor Philip Morrison of MIT] said one time that you people did not see the target, that the reason you dropped the bomb, like you said, verboten, against the rules, regulations, was so that you wouldn't have to fly back to Tinian with the bomb on board.

We could not have flown back to Tinian with the bomb on board because we didn't have enough fuel and therefore we landed on Okinawa and just barely made it. But, I think sometimes our memories are dimmed a little by these things, especially if one wasn't precisely there. . . . But we did not see the ground until, I would say, within ten seconds of the release and I remember Beechan saying, "I've got it! I've got it!" and bingo, it was gone. And when 10,000 pounds leaves an airplane, that leaves a big void, and the airplane takes a big jump. I knew it was gone.

This caller, a bomb buff, continued the inquiry. "But did you see the target, in effect?" General Sweeney satisfied his curiosity. "In the last ten seconds, I did not. The bombardier did."

The general answered every question, patiently and in detail, frequently pausing to refresh his memory so that he could give a precise answer. One caller was interested in his fuel supply.

We had three reasons for running low on fuel. Just before takeoff on the final check, I found that one of my 600-gallon tanks in the rear bomb bay . . . we have two bomb bays. We had tanks in the rear bomb bay. And one of my 600-gallon tanks in there was not feeding. There was what we call a faulty solenoid. It just wouldn't open a valve and permit it to feed the main system. So I was reduced from 7,000 total to a usable 6,400 and, therefore, from a reserve of 1,000 to a reserve of 400. I jumped out of the airplane. I talked to Paul Tibbets, who was my boss, and he was standing there, and I asked him. He said, "What do you want to do?" I said, "I want to go." He said, "Go." So the decision was made just like that. But then I had to fight weather on the route. I had to fly at 17,000 feet instead of at low altitude on route because of the weather. I had to rendezvous at 30,000 feet instead of at 8,000 feet, all of which took more fuel. Four runs on Kokura took more fuel.

You made four passes at Kokura trying to see the target and it never happened?

Right.

And you made one at Nagasaki, and, by God, you were going to get rid of that bomb!

Well, if we didn't have a good radar fix on it I would have made another run.

The host transformed the general's workaday details into heroic struggle: "By God, you were going to get rid of that bomb!" But the workaday details are what interested the callers, people apparently more interested in mechanics than in morality.

Some callers asked about alternative targets. Three were interested in the height at which the bomb was dropped and the height at which it exploded. Several asked about the structure of the bomb—height, weight, metallurgy, circumference, composition. One knowledgeable caller asked several highly technical questions about the trigger mechanism. One caller inquired about the impact of the explosion on General Sweeney's plane. Several inquiries were directed to what the crew could see of the explosion and the ensuing destruction. The callers wanted to know about the engineering of the bomb and the problems of delivery. There were less interested in the feelings of the pilot and his crew, and little concerned with the carnage. Their paramount interest was the state of the destructive art.

The questions were not merely about mechanics and logistics. Callers wanted to know the details, and General Sweeney provided them. The questions were not merely about weather, they were about cloud formation visibility, visibility at different altitudes and locations, weather and alternative targets, orders as affected by visibility, cloud cover, weather and the use of radar, and cloud cover as it affected bombarding. General Sweeney fed this hunger: "Over Nagasaki was 6/10–8/10 puffy summer clouds, at base 8,000, at top about 10."

The human issue got lost in a discussion of weather conditions, fuel, radar, altitude, visibility, and so on. These variables became the only reality. Neither the callers nor the general spoke of those killed or maimed by the bomb. The victims appeared to be irrelevant. The cloud cover, the trigger mechanism, and the weight of the bomb were real. But the citizens of Nagasaki were not mentioned.

General Sweeney was eager to justify the bombing. He provided a rationalization that made the bombing appear to be merely a practical decision, a calculation of moral and military benefits.

I'd like to take it one step at a time. The first part is, should we, or should we not, have tried to win the war? I think the answer for both you and me is that we were fighting nations who were plundering and rapacious. And I'd like to talk about Japan for a moment. They had tortured all of greater East Asia. They had stolen everything they could.

They had raped and tortured in China. They were torturing Americans in the prison camps.

General Sweeeny interrupted his calendar of Japanese crimes for a moment to comment on the "lawfulness" of the Germans.

Germans went at least somewhat by Geneva Convention. The Japanese paid no attention to it. The Japanese could have quit any time they wanted. I am going to read a little note that I have in front of me here. It says, quote, "President Truman was in Potsdam conferring with Marshall Stalin, Prime Minister Churchill and later Prime Minister Clement Attlee." Now this was in July of 1945, before the atomic bombs and after the end of the war in Europe. Now we continue to quote, "From this meeting emerged the Potsdam ultimatum, the document that demanded Japan's unconditional surrender or promised her a reign of ruin." Continue quote, "The terms of the Potsdam ultimatum were made known to Japan." Still, she dickered. It was at this point [we] bolted into action. Something tremendous was about to happen, and it did.

Now, I believe in God and I don't believe there should ever be any war of any kind, but I say that if we are being attacked by a rotten group of warmongers and we are in a legal war and the president asks you and me to do it, we damn well better do it. We hear a lot about the victims of the war in Japan and in other parts of the world in World War II, but we never hear anything about the victims at Pearl Harbor. Are we such bad guys that we forget our own dead?

I would say that war should never occur, but neither then perhaps, by the same token, if we were not to have used the weapons we used, and let me say that for the next five years until Russia got them, the world was at peace because we controlled them. As long as the United States controlled them, the world was at peace. And it was only when the Russians got them that wars started again: Korea, Vietnam, etc., and many others, Afghani-

stan, for example. So, as long as we are strong, we will
not be attacked.

The host broke in, "So, you are not convinced by the freezeniks?"
General Sweeney supplied the expected answer, "No, not at all. I
respect their opinions, but, in my opinion, to which I am entitled,
is that only when we become weak or weaker, will we be attacked."
    The morality of the mission is lost in the details of cost analysis.
The host was preoccupied with the nuclear freeze movement.

Take it in the current question, which has nothing to do
with Lebanon, but does have to do with the nuclear freeze,
and it almost has become a religious rite, that on the
anniversary of the bombing of Hiroshima, they have, that
people have vigils, they talk to victims, they try to make
it sound as if (a) that was a terrible thing, and, of course,
it was terrible in the destructive power but terrible in the
sense that it shouldn't have been done. And (b) that somehow the United States should be held to account for ever
using a nuclear bomb and that nuclear warfare should be
abolished and the nuclear arsenal should be dismantled.
When you hear, not only the mood, but the tone, what
do you think?

Well, no strong nation has ever been attacked. We were
attacked at Pearl Harbor because we were weak.

The details become the brick and mortar upon which the edifice
of legend is built. And the legend becomes a celebration, a sacred
act, memorialized in the reunions of heroic warriors who forged it.
The moral dimension is lost in the consuming interest in technical
matters, both because the bomb was dropped in 1945—thirty-seven
years before these conversations occurred—and because during the
intervening time no other bomb has been dropped on human beings.
Memory fades, and with it, impact. Hannah Arendt's description of
Adolph Eichmann as an exemplar of the "banality of evil," the horrendous perceived as the commonplace, might characterize the bomb
group. Extermination took place at a distance. The plane that delivered the bomb was remote from the target. The distance enhances

the abstract quality of the victims, and permits a memory of the event in which victims are not perceived as persons.[1] Americans acknowledge a long tradition of domestic violence.

The raid on Nagasaki is the ultimate Western, a quintessential American triumph of good over evil, the triumph of courage and technology over the recalcitrant forces of sadistic bullies. General Sweeney participated in the heroic tradition of the frontier: the U.S. Cavalry decimating the Indian and restoring peace to the countryside. The hero overcomes enormous odds, displays his manhood, never doubts the mission, goes to the brink, is almost defeated, and then triumphs. Death and transfiguration are the themes; heroism and loyalty are the counterpoints. The caller reaffirms the epic with a classic Hollywood line, "By God, you were going to get rid of that bomb!"

The genocidal act is lost in the technological triumph and the Wagnerian heroics. The triumph is very American. The issue is technique and manhood, not morality. The issue is engineering and guts, not murder.

The American tradition is pragmatic and the grandeur of that tradition is manifest in mechanical, electrical, and aeronautical invention. The cotton gin, the telephone, the reaper, the phonograph, the automobile, the airplane, and the computer are America's triumphs over nature. Thomas Edison, the Wright brothers, and Henry Ford epitomize this pragmatic tradition. They are the romantic heroes of a more innocent epoch. The inventor-genius working in solitude against great odds and with little money—the master tinkerer—becomes the folk hero, perhaps a bit less statuesque than Lou Gehrig and Babe Ruth. Their entry into the adolescent's pantheon of gods was facilitated by the fact that they fulfilled the dream of Horatio Alger. Good fortune accompanied Mr. Ford and Mr. Edison.

The admiration for mechanical invention carried over to the American home. The basement full of tools and the amateur's knowledge of automotive parts and engines, of carpentry and plumbing, was at one time an American staple. Tinkering is an American tradition, a talent worthy of the neighbors' admiration, and a source of pride. Although the bomb was a triumph of theoretical physics performed on the highest level by the most accomplished minds, the callers perceived it as an enterprise in high-class popular mechanics, the zenith of tinkering. They were not concerned with fission or fusion, but with mechanics: the trigger mechanism, the shape and weight of the bomb. The bomb as technique becomes the ultimate metaphor for America.

In this yearning for intimacy, detail, nuance, climax, and secrets, is there a displaced voyeurism, a masked sexual inquiry, a peek at the ultimate in discipline and bondage? Perhaps, but the bombing is also the metaphor for conflict between good and evil, civilization and barbarism, international law and order and its defilement, occidental and oriental—perhaps these are the dichotomies that excite. Framing the nuclear bomb issue in these terms permits the conqueror to accept mass slaughter while believing that every life has value.

Note

1. Philip Slater, *The Pursuit of Loneliness* (Boston: The Beacon Press, 1970), ch. 2.

Index

About the Author

MURRAY LEVIN is a professor of political science at Boston University. He received his undergraduate degree from Harvard College and his doctorate from Columbia University. He has pursued the twin themes of political alienation and represssion in America for three decades. *Talk Radio and the American Dream* amplifies this theme by analyzing the substantial mistrust of America that developed in the 1960s and 1970s.

Professor Levin is the author of *The Alienated Voter: Politics in Boston; The Compleat Politician: Political Strategy in Massachusetts; Kennedy Campaigning: The System and Style as Practiced by Senator Kennedy; Political Hysteria in America: The Democratic Capacity for Repression;* and *Edward Kennedy: The Myth of Leadership.*